# Fundamentals of
# Trading Energy
# Futures & Options

## 2nd Edition

# Fundamentals of
# Trading Energy
# Futures & Options
## 2ND EDITION

BY STEVEN ERRERA
D STEWART L. BROWN

Copyright© 2002
PennWell Corporation
1421 S. Sheridan
Tulsa, OK 74112
800-752-9764
sales@pennwell.com
www.pennwell-store.com
www.pennwell.com

*cover and book design by Brigitte Coffman*

**Library of Congress Cataloging-in-Publication data available on request.**

Errera, Steven
    Fundamentals of trading energy futures and options / Errera, Steven
Brown, Stewart L.–2nd editon.
    p. cm.
    q.cm
    Includes index
    ISBN 0-87814-836-1

Printed in the United States of America.

3    4    5    06    05    04

# Contents

# Figures

# Tables

# Acknowledgments

Every book requires special expertise from a variety of sources. For this second edition, I again want to thank the staff members of the New York Mercantile Exchange (NYMEX), the International Petroleum Exchange (IPE), the Kansas City Board of Trade, the Chicago Board of Trade, the Minneapolis Grain Exchange, and the Futures Industry Association who provided needed information, with a special thank you to the NYMEX statistical department, Dan Brusstar and Dan McElduff from NYMEX research, and the staff of the IPE. I'd also like to thank Walt Usatschew, Brad McKenzie, and Mitch Barber from the petroleum industry.

Last but not least, thank you again, my wonderful wife, Edie Korotkin, for your valuable assistance in the preparation of this new edition, and on whose support I always rely.

*Steven Errera*

# Introduction

Trading in energy futures and options contracts is changing the manner in which energy related firms operate. Although agricultural commodity futures contracts have been trading for well over 120 years, the first successful energy futures contract was introduced in 1978. It was a contract that called for the delivery of heating oil. Since that initial success, energy-related futures and options contracts have achieved steady growth. In addition to heating oil, natural gas, crude oil, gasoline, propane, gas oil, and electricity contracts are trading.

The success of energy futures and options contracts is not surprising since futures markets present many opportunities to reduce risk and enhance profitability. A solid understanding of how energy futures and options markets work, and how energy futures and options contracts may be used in the energy business, will pay large dividends to those firms willing to invest the time and energy necessary to master these techniques.

The purpose of this book is to explain the fundamentals of energy futures and options markets in a manner that is both correct and understandable. Unfortunately, there is a large amount of misinformation concerning these markets, which is routinely accepted as gospel. In addition to providing a solid grounding in futures and options markets, it is our goal to dispel some of these myths.

Throughout the book we use energy futures market-related examples. However, virtually all of the information presented generalizes readily to all futures and options contracts and markets. In chapter 1 we present an overview of energy futures and options contracts and markets. Chapter 2 is entitled "Market Mechanics" and presents much useful information on the operation of energy futures markets. Chapter 3 covers the behavior of futures contract prices and the very important relationships between cash and futures prices. Chapter 4 covers speculation and techniques of profiting on relative price changes by using spreads.

Perhaps the most useful information in the book is contained in chapter 5, which covers hedging techniques. Hedging is the primary way that energy-related firms may benefit from futures markets. Hedging techniques are risk-reducing techniques that also offer the potential to increase profits. Chapter 6 introduces the concepts of options on futures contracts and chapter 7 explains various energy options strategies. Chapter 8 briefly covers technical analysis and chapter 9 covers the history and growth of energy futures and options markets. Finally, chapter 10 covers the benefits of futures and options in general and looks into the future of energy futures markets with a discussion of how such markets will impact on energy-related firms and the general public.

In addition to the above materials, we present a summary of the rules of the most active energy futures and options contracts. These include heating oil, crude oil, natural gas, unleaded gasoline, propane, coal, Palo Verde electricity, California–Oregon Border electricity, Cinergy electricity and Entergy electricity contracts traded on the New York Mercantile Exchange; and gas oil, Brent crude oil and natural gas contracts traded on the International Petroleum Exchange. A comprehensive glossary of commodity futures and energy industry terms is also included.

# Futures and Options Contracts and Markets

Commodity futures contracts are legally binding and negotiable contracts that call for the delivery of agricultural, industrial,
or financial commodities in the future, hence the term "futures
contract." Options are also legally binding and negotiable contracts
that give the holder the right, but not the obligation, to purchase
or sell the underlying futures contract at a specified price and time
for a one-time premium payment. Futures and options contracts
are traded on futures and options markets, which are composed
of exchanges and brokers that facilitate the buying and selling of
contracts. Commodity futures and options markets are central
marketplaces, located primarily in Chicago and New York,
although recently markets have developed in such diversified
locales as London, Tokyo, Beijing, Frankfurt, Paris, and São Paolo.
Today there are more than sixty marketplaces worldwide where
trading in futures or options contracts occurs.

Futures markets are primarily financial markets that trade
commodity futures and options contracts. Even though futures contracts may involve actual delivery of physical commodities, such
delivery is a relatively rare occurrence in mature futures markets.

Commodity futures markets in the United States, Canada,
Europe, and Asia serve an important economic function. The
markets facilitate the transfer of risk among various market

participants and in the process reduce risk for producers and processors and improve the flow of commerce.

Commodity futures contracts are traded for a variety of commodities. Agricultural commodities such as wheat and corn have been traded in Chicago since about 1860. During the last fifty years futures contracts have been developed for industrial commodities such as platinum and copper. There are also well-developed futures markets for foreign currencies such as the British pound and the Japanese yen. Contracts on financial instruments such as treasury bonds and Eurodollars are dramatically changing the financial system, while futures contracts on stock indexes and options on commodity futures are dramatically increasing risk-reduction alternatives for commerce.

Yet, the most exciting development in recent years was the introduction of contracts in energy products such as heating oil, crude oil, gasoline, natural gas, and electricity. Energy futures contracts are enhancing the operation of the petroleum distribution system and changing the way petroleum is priced worldwide. A complete list of actively traded energy futures contracts is presented in Table 1–1 and a list of actively traded energy options contracts is presented in Table 1–2.

| Contract | Market | Delivery Point |
|----------|--------|----------------|
| Crude Oil | New York | Cushing, Oklahoma |
| Natural Gas | New York | Henry Hub, Louisiana |
| Brent Crude Oil | London | EFP/Cash Settlement |
| No. 2 Heating Oil | New York | New York Harbor |
| Unleaded Regular Gasoline | New York | New York Harbor |
| Gas Oil | London | A.R.A. Area |
| Natural Gas | London | UK NPB |

**Table 1–1** Energy Futures Contracts Trading More Than 100,000 Contracts/Year

Participants in futures markets may be classified under two broad categories: commercials and noncommercials (also known as speculators). Commercials are those market participants who own or will own actual commodities and are motivated to use futures markets to reduce the risk of price variation in those commodities. This is called hedging. Noncommercials, or speculators, seek price variation risk and in the process attempt to profit from it. This is called speculation. Futures markets are arenas where risk is transferred among market participants.

| Option | Market |
|---|---|
| Crude Oil | New York |
| Natural Gas | New York |
| No. 2 Heating Oil | New York |
| Unleaded Regular Gasoline | New York |
| Brent Crude Oil | London |
| Gas Oil | London |

**Table 1–2** Energy Options Contracts Trading More Than 50,000 Options/Year

Hedging refers to any action taken to reduce risk. Hedging in commodity futures markets is undertaken to reduce the risk of price fluctuations. An example of this kind of price risk is the risk the refiner faces because he does not know when he purchases crude oil what the market price will be for gasoline, heating oil, and residual oil 30 or 60 days later. Another example is the risk the heating oil distributor faces when he contracts with his customers to deliver fuel oil at a fixed price but doesn't know ahead of time at what price he will be able to purchase the heating oil. Changes in the cash or spot market prices of various agricultural and industrial commodities and financial instruments can be hedged in futures markets.

Risk reduction is accomplished by assuming a futures position opposite to the position the hedger has in the underlying commodity. The position in the actual physical commodity is known as a "cash" or "spot" market position. The terms are used interchangeably. The combination of the cash and futures positions causes price changes to cancel, and the resultant net position is one in which price changes are reduced or eliminated. This is the essence of hedging.

The opportunity to hedge price risk is valuable to the firm because it allows the firm that hedges to focus on business concerns rather than expending time and energy attempting to forecast prices. Because risk is reduced, the hedger can typically afford to operate on narrower but more certain margins. In some instances, profitability is actually increased. In general, by reducing price uncertainty, hedging improves the flow of commerce and ultimately results in lower and more stable prices to the consumer.

Speculators are motivated by profits to participate in futures markets. In the process they perform the economic functions of assuming risk and providing liquidity to the market. The speculator hopes to profit from price changes of various agricultural and other commodities. Speculators use various types of analysis to forecast prices and price changes. They buy when they think prices are too low and sell when they think prices are too high. This contributes to the efficient pricing of commodities in the future and provides liquidity to the futures market. One of the most important functions of futures markets is to provide the public with information about the prices of commodities. Petroleum products are traded worldwide, and there are many different prices of product depending on grade and location. Futures markets provide a central marketplace and a centrally determined reference price, which can be used to price product worldwide. This is called "price discovery" and is one of the major benefits of futures markets.

The business world has become increasingly aware of futures markets and especially of energy futures markets. The introduction of contracts on financial instruments, energy, and stock indexes has dramatically increased the range of potential users of futures markets. In addition, changes in the business climate, OPEC (Organization of Petroleum Exporting Countries), deregulation of the energy industry, fluctuating interest rates, and governmental monetary and fiscal policies have greatly increased the risks of doing business. Participation in futures markets has been growing dramatically and is expected to accelerate in the future. The introduction, in the mid 1980s, of commodity options contracts has also contributed to the rapid growth of futures markets. As business people become more familiar with the workings of futures markets, hedging should become a more common business practice. Familiarity with futures markets and hedging techniques will become a necessity for all businesses that are subject to price risk.

# COMMODITY FUTURES AND OPTIONS CONTRACTS AND MARKETS

Hedging and speculating in commodity futures markets is accomplished by trading commodity futures contracts. A commodity futures contract is a contract to make or take delivery of a standardized amount of a specific quality of a commodity at a specified time in the future.

Energy futures and options contracts are traded for all 12 delivery months, sometimes as far as 7 years in the future. The prices of futures and options contracts are determined by a highly competitive auction process on commodity futures exchanges. The majority of energy contracts are traded on the New York Mercantile Exchange (NYMEX) and the International Petroleum Exchange (IPE) in London. Agricultural and financial futures contracts and options are traded primarily in Chicago on the Chicago Board of Trade (CBOT) and the Chicago Mercantile Exchange (CME). There are other exchanges that trade contracts on various commodities in New York and in other parts of the country. There are also almost 50 exchanges outside the United States that trade in futures or options contracts, although most of their trading volume consists of financial contracts.

The prices of futures contracts for any particular delivery month often change sharply from day to day and week to week depending on numerous developments that influence market prices. Prices often change when there is news of factors that will influence the supply and demand for the underlying commodity in the future. For energy-related commodities, factors such as weather conditions, OPEC pricing policies, forecast gasoline consumption, and a myriad of technical and other factors will cause the prices of futures contracts to change. The prices of commodity futures contracts are determined in a highly efficient central marketplace and at any point in time prices reflect the market's best estimate of the correct price of the commodity given all of the factors that are known to have an impact on the current and future level of energy prices.

Futures contracts involve a contractual obligation by both parties to either make or take delivery of the underlying commodity. Physical delivery of the underlying commodity is always possible with futures contracts. However, futures contracts recently have been introduced which call for cash settlement rather than physical delivery. An example of this is the stock index futures contract where delivery of the several hundred different stocks that comprise the stock index would be impossible.

Actual delivery is quite rare. Less than 2% of all futures contracts traded result in actual physical delivery. It is more common that the contractual obligation to make or take delivery is satisfied by selling a similar contract in the futures market. This is called an "offset."

An offset occurs when the holder of a commodity futures position assumes another position opposite to the original position. Because there is now an obligation to both buy and sell, the exchange allows the two positions to offset each other and thus the obligation to make or take delivery is satisfied. Of course, the trader assumes financial responsibility for the difference in price between the two positions. Thus, because there is a ready and liquid market to buy or sell futures contracts, commodity futures markets are able to act principally as financial markets. The exchanges are public in the sense that anyone who makes the necessary arrangements with member brokerage firms can trade. The ability to satisfy the obligation on a futures contract by offsetting means, for example, that speculators don't have to be in the heating oil business to trade heating oil futures contracts or in the propane business to trade propane futures.

Like the financial market for stocks and bonds, futures markets are international in scope and regulated to insure the smooth and honest fulfillment of trades. Perhaps because of the regulated nature of these markets, the record for legal and ethical operation is excellent.

It is the ability to offset futures positions in futures markets that allows hedgers in all areas of the world to hedge. The refiner in Illinois, the heating oil distributor in Maine, or the electric consumer in California can use the futures market to hedge even though there is no intent to make or take delivery on the contract. Indeed, in most cases transportation costs are prohibitive. Financial transactions take place via telephone and there is no necessity to ship commodities to and from remote delivery points. Typically, hedgers will offset their futures positions at the same time that they eliminate cash market positions in local cash markets.

## Historical development

Futures markets in their present form came into existence about 120 years ago but the principles involved have been used for hundreds of years. The first recorded instance of contracting for goods in the future at a fixed price occurred during the time of the Phoenicians. Standardized futures contracts on rice were traded in Japan in the middle of the 18th century.

In the United States, trading of futures contracts developed from the practice of forward contracting. In the early 1800s farm surpluses were generated and brought to market in the Chicago area. However, because of the seasonal nature of farming and livestock production, the farmer often faced chaotic market conditions. Around harvest time, processors had more than adequate supplies and, having little storage capabilities, would bid very low prices. Often goods were left in the streets to spoil because of a lack of any demand at all. A few months later, supplies would disappear and prices would increase dramatically.

The forward contract was developed in response to this chaotic situation. Like a futures contract, a forward contract is a legal agreement to make or take delivery in the future. A farmer could contract with a food processor or transport company to sell his goods at a fixed price near harvest time. The ability to contract with a buyer at a fixed price in the future sharply reduced the farmer's risk. The ability of the processor to contract for a supply of grain or livestock in the future at a fixed price reduced his risk as well.

The ability to guarantee sources of supply and demand ahead of time, along with the resultant reduction of uncertainty, contributed greatly to the development of the middlemen, transportation, and storage facilities necessary for the smooth flow of product from producers to ultimate consumers.

Forward contracting became common in the 1830s. In 1848, the Chicago Board of Trade was founded as an association by a group of 82 men representing various business interests. Both cash trading and forward contracts were traded on the CBOT at the same time. Eventually, forward contracts were standardized and became futures contracts as we know them. This occurred around the time of the Civil War.

# Comparison of forward and futures contracts

Forward and futures contracts are similar in that they both involve an element of futurity. Forward contracts, also known as cash forward contracts, are cash or spot market transactions in which the parties agree to the purchase and sale of the commodity at some future time under agreed-upon conditions. Each forward contract is a unique legal instrument that is tailor-made to suit each particular situation. Thus, forward contracts are not standardized and are usually not transferable except with the consent of the other party, often for some consideration. Delivery is typical in forward contracting and the market is geographically dispersed. It is primarily a telephone market made by major dealers, and the time periods involved are relatively short.

In contrast, futures contracts are completely standardized. The terms of each contract (natural gas, crude oil, gasoline, wheat, gold, etc.) on a particular exchange are the same in all respects except price. Futures contracts are readily transferable with only a small transaction cost. The commodity exchange provides a mechanism whereby contracts may be purchased or sold.

With forward contracting there is typically an element of concern regarding the ability of the parties to perform on the contract. This is called "default risk." In futures contracts there is no such concern because the futures exchange places itself between the buyer and seller of each futures contract. Once the agents for the buyer and seller meet on the floor of the exchange and negotiate the price, all connection between the buyer and seller is severed. The exchange becomes the buyer's seller and the seller's buyer so that the solvency of a particular transaction as far as the parties are concerned is dependent only upon the solvency of the exchange involved. Default is very rare in organized futures markets.

It is not unusual for forward and futures markets to exist for the same commodity. A good example of this coexistence is the market for foreign currencies, also known as foreign exchange. Large multinational banks operate foreign exchange departments for the convenience of their customers. They trade currencies for both immediate delivery and for delivery in the future (forward contracts). In the forward market, delivery will typically take place, although it is usually possible to assign the rights of a forward contract to third parties. As previously mentioned, there are also completely standardized futures contracts for foreign exchange traded in futures markets.

# COMMODITY FUTURES EXCHANGES

Until recently, all commodity futures exchanges in the United States have been not-for-profit membership associations. Each association limits the number of individuals that may become members. Every membership, called a "seat" on the exchange, is owned by an individual. In certain instances, companies, partnerships, and cooperatives may be registered for certain membership privileges. The New York Mercantile Exchange (NYMEX) and the Chicago Mercantile Exchange (CME) have recently become for-profit corporations of which the members are stockholders. The International Petroleum Exchange (IPE) in Europe has also converted to a for-profit corporation.

Exchange members may be placed in three broad categories. Some members represent commercial interests that are primarily engaged in the producing, marketing, or processing of commodities and use the market to hedge against price risk. Others may speculate for their own accounts. A third group, called brokers, executes orders for individuals, partnerships, and corporations that are not members of the exchange. Some members may engage in all three activities at one time or another. Nonmembers trade through brokerage firms, which hold memberships through partners or officers. The exchanges are supported by dues and assessments on members as well as exchange fees on each transaction on the exchange.

Each exchange member must meet certain standards of financial responsibility, credit standing, and character. The exchanges are self-regulating. Members elect a board in which is vested the power to promulgate rules, create committees, hire staff, discipline members, and so on.

The world's oldest and largest commodity futures exchange, the Chicago Board of Trade, was founded in 1848. The New York Mercantile Exchange, also known as the energy exchange, is the third oldest exchange and was founded in 1872. It has 816 memberships and a board of directors and several standing committees charged with various responsibilities.

Exchange members buy and sell contracts on the floor of the exchange. Trading is conducted in trading areas called "pits" which are generally octagonal in shape and are made up of a series of steps on which the brokers and traders stand, all facing one another. There is a different pit for each type of contract being traded, but the method of trading is the same in all pits. Every offer to buy or sell a contract must be called or cried out publicly, resulting in a process that appears to an outsider to be total bedlam amid chaos. Open outcry is supplemented by hand signals.

Exchange members may trade for their own accounts, in which case they may be hedgers or speculators, or they may execute orders for hedgers and speculators located off the floor of the exchange. In these cases members are acting as brokers and receive commissions for their efforts. Strict exchange rules require that members acting as brokers place the interests of customers before their own interests.

Associated with each exchange is a clearing corporation or clearinghouse. It performs all clerical and financial tasks involved with keeping track of the thousands of trades that occur on the floor of the exchange each day. Each trade must be cleared through the clearinghouse. For each futures contract there is a chain of financial responsibility from the buyer or seller to the brokerage firm to the clearing corporation.

The New York Mercantile Exchange owns and operates its own clearinghouse where all the trading positions are fully margined and marked to market at the end of each day. The International Petroleum Exchange in London clears its trades through the London Clearing House (LCH). The LCH is able to guarantee contract performance by the collection of a margin payable on any outstanding position at the end of each day, calculated according to the value of that position.

Although not all members of the exchange are members of the clearinghouse, each exchange member must clear his trades through a clearing member. Each clearing member has funds on deposit with the clearinghouse. These funds serve as a guarantee that the member has the financial means to support his trading activities.

In addition to individual members, brokerage firms are members of the clearinghouse of each exchange. The brokerage firms in turn require that their customers who trade futures contracts also maintain margins against their futures contracts.

# ELECTRONIC TRADING

During the 1980s, the combination of the technological revolution and the increasingly competitive nature of world business encouraged futures exchanges to reach out beyond their normal borders and time zones in the form of electronic trading. Some exchanges used electronic trading as their only trading medium, while others used it to expand their traditional floor trading day. In 1993, the New York Mercantile Exchange introduced after-hours trading with its NYMEX ACCESS℠ system which effectively extended the trading day to almost a full 24 hours. At present, the International Petroleum Exchange has electronic trading from 8:00 A.M. to 9:00 A.M., but will expand to a fully electronic trading system in 2002.

# REGULATION

In the United States, the major regulatory provisions regarding commodity futures contracts are contained in the Commodity Exchange Act (CEA) which is enforced and administered by an independent governmental regulatory commission called the Commodity Futures Trading Commission (CFTC).

Futures trading may be conducted only on exchanges officially designated by the CFTC. The markets so designated must comply with certain stipulations of the CEA and the rules and regulations issued and administered by the CFTC. The CEA also forbids cheating, defrauding, dissemination of false information, and manipulation.

The National Futures Association (NFA), authorized by an act of Congress, is the futures industry's first industry-wide self-regulatory organization. The NFA is responsible for the registration of futures professionals, arbitration, auditing, and other duties as they develop.

# Market Mechanics

## LONG AND SHORT POSITIONS

A futures contract is a legally binding agreement to make or take delivery of a commodity in the future. There are two parties to every contract—one party agrees to buy and take delivery in the future and the other party agrees to sell and make delivery in the future. The party that agrees to buy and take delivery has what is referred to as a long position. This party is called the buyer and is said to have bought a contract. The party that agrees to sell and make delivery has what is referred to as a short position. The short is also called the seller and is said to have sold a contract.

The terms long and short are also used with regard to spot market commodity positions as well as in the stock and bond markets. The general notion of a long position is that profits are made when prices increase and losses occur when prices decrease. With a short position profits occur when prices decrease and losses occur when prices increase. The profit or loss on a short position is thus opposite to the profit or loss on a long position.

For instance, assume a trader buys a heating oil contract that calls for the delivery of 42,000 gallons of heating oil. The price of the contract is $1 per gallon. The total value of his position is $1 x 42,000 gallons, or $42,000. If the price of the futures contract should increase to $1.015 per gallon, the contract would be worth $1.015 x 42,000, or $42,630. The price has increased and the buyer has profited by $630 which is the $.015 per gallon increase multiplied by 42,000 gallons. If the price of the contract had decreased to $.995, the total value of the contract would be $41,790 and the buyer of the contract would have lost $210.

The profits and losses resulting from selling a contract (short position) are opposite those of the long position. In the previous example, where the price increases by $.015 the contract seller would lose $630 and where the price decreases by $.005 the contract seller would gain $210.

Because there is a long contract outstanding for every short contract, it is always so that for every winner in the commodity futures market there is also a loser. Gains and losses in the market always net out and the exchange itself is unaffected when prices increase or decrease. Thus, commodity futures contracts are what is called a zero-sum game.

In commodity futures markets, long and short positions are assumed with equal ease and there is no impediment placed on short positions. (In the stock markets, the short selling mechanism is subject to institutional constraints such as interest, extra margin requirements, and responsibility for dividends.) In addition, there is no stigma attached to going short in futures markets as there sometimes is in the stock market.

The concept of long and short positions is similar in the cash or spot market. A long position in the cash market is the same as owning the physical commodity; such a position is known as a long cash position. The gasoline distributor who has product stored as inventory has a long cash position; his inventory value increases when cash prices increase and decreases when cash prices decrease. A less obvious long cash position is that of the farmer who will harvest grain in the future. Because he will own grain in the future, he will profit if prices increase and will lose if prices decrease; that is, he is subject to price risk.

Similarly, it is possible to be short in the cash market. Suppose a gasoline distributor contracts with customers to deliver gasoline in the future at a fixed price. The distributor does not know ahead of time at what price he will be able to purchase the gasoline. If gasoline prices should increase, the distributor will find that his costs have increased and that his profit margin has decreased. If gasoline prices decrease his profit margin increases. The distributor has a short position in the cash market. The gasoline distributor in the second example is subject to price risk just as the distributor in the first example was subject to price risk. The only difference is that their profit positions change inversely when prices change.

# MARGIN REQUIREMENTS

Recall the example of the speculator who purchased a 42,000 gallon heating oil futures contract at $1 per gallon. The total value of heating oil under contract was $42,000. At the time the contract was purchased, no actual money changed hands between the makers of the contract. All financial dealings with the commodity exchanges are through their clearinghouses. Exchanges require that buyers and sellers of contracts deposit and maintain funds as a guarantee of performance on the contract. This is called margin.

Margin as a performance guarantee in futures markets is conceptually different from margin in the stock market. In the stock market, margin is a type of down payment where the balance of the stock purchased is financed by borrowed funds.

There are two types of margin on futures contracts: initial margin and maintenance, or variation, margin. Initial margin requirements are fixed dollar amounts, which are typically between 5 and 10% of the value of the commodity under contract. Table 2–1 presents the margin requirements for the energy futures contracts currently traded on the New York Mercantile Exchange.

| Commodity | Initial Minimum Margins* |
|---|---|
| Crude Oil (1,000 bbls.) | $2,025 |
| Natural Gas (10,000 MMBtu) | $3,105 |
| Heating Oil (42,000 gals.) | $2,025 |
| Unleaded Regular Gasoline (42,000 gals.) | $2,025 |
| Propane (42,000 gals.) | $1,620 |
| Palo Verde Electricity (432 Mwh) | $2,700 |
| California-Oregon Border Electricity (432 Mwh) | $2,025 |
| Cinergy Electricity (736 Mwh) | $4,050 |
| Entergy Electricity (736 Mwh) | $4,050 |

(*Brokerage firms may impose higher margins than the exchanges, and margin requirements change from time to time.)

**Table 2–1** Margin Requirements for New York Mercantile Exchange Energy Futures Contracts

Initial margin requirements are determined by the exchange and are updated periodically when factors such as price volatility and contract value change. Initial margins serve as a good-faith deposit for the execution of the contract.

In addition to initial margins, exchanges have maintenance margins, also known as variation margins, which are typically between 60 and 85% of the initial margin. The concept of maintenance margin is that when a contract suffers losses to the point that margin has decreased to 60 to 85% of initial margin, the trader will receive a margin call and be required to deposit additional margin money to bring the account equity up to the initial margin requirement. Should the customer fail to deposit the additional money, the brokerage firm will liquidate the position.

Lower initial margin is required for commercial or trade accounts. These are non-speculative, hedging accounts where the net worth of the hedger is likely to be high and the possibility of default correspondingly low. Brokerage firms frequently require slightly higher initial and maintenance margins than the exchanges. There are also lower margin requirements for what are called spreads or straddles (see chapter 4).

Each of the brokerage firm's customers has a margin account that reflects all contracts purchased and sold by the customer. Each account is adjusted at the end of every day for both realized and unrealized gains and losses. This is called marking to market. This is done in order to assure that each account has sufficient equity to comply with margin requirements and thus perform financially on all contract obligations. If realized and unrealized gains exceed realized and unrealized losses, then equity will increase and the trader may either withdraw funds or use the excess to margin more contracts. If losses exceed gains, then equity will decrease and the trader may receive a margin call.

Brokerage firms must also settle each day with the clearinghouses of the exchanges with which they deal. Settlement with exchanges takes the form of a delivery or receipt of a certified check or federal funds for the amount of net realized and unrealized gains and losses on all the firm's customers' initial cash positions. Thus, there is a clear channel of financial responsibility from the customer to the brokerage firm to the clearinghouse. The procedure of marking to market daily maintains the integrity of the futures marketplace.

Brokerage firms typically require a minimum equity of $10,000 to open a commodity trading account. Consider the speculator who purchased the 42,000 gallon heating oil contract at $1 per gallon. The total value of heating oil under the contract was $42,000. His margin requirement on the contract might be $2,025 and his maintenance margin would be $1,500. If, on the day following the purchase, heating oil closed at $1.015 per gallon, an increase of $.015 per gallon, the speculator would have profited by $630 and his equity would increase from $2,025 to $2,655 (ignoring any other equity in the account). This $630 could be withdrawn from the account or used to margin other contracts.

If the price of the heating oil contract decreased to $.98, the speculator would receive a margin call (again ignoring any other equity in the account). The value of the contract decreased by $.02 per gallon or a total of $840. This leaves $1,185 as margin, which is less than the $1,500 maintenance margin. The speculator would be required to deposit enough additional equity ($840) to bring the account back up to the original margin requirement ($2,025). As a practical matter, treasury bills are often deposited to meet initial margin requirements so that the trader earns some return on the funds deposited.

Short positions are also marked to market on a daily basis. Equity is increased when prices decrease and vice versa.

It is the net equity position on contracts which have not been offset in the account that is used to calculate maintenance margins. Thus, a trader may have unrealized losses on some heating oil futures contracts which are offset by gains in crude oil futures contracts. There would be no margin call as long as the net equity position of all contracts in the account is greater than the maintenance margin requirement.

Futures contracts are attractive to speculators because margin requirements are low in relation to the total value of the contract. With low margin requirements, speculators are able to achieve a high degree of leverage. Recall the example of the speculator. When the price of the contract increased 1.5% from $1 to $1.015, the speculator's equity increased about 31%, from $2,025 to $2,655. Of course, leverage is a two-edged sword; it works in the other direction also. This makes futures contracts potentially very profitable but also very risky. It is possible for adverse price moves to completely wipe out a trader's equity within a very short time period.

Hedging accounts are also marked to market on a daily basis. However, margin requirements are lower on hedging accounts than on speculative accounts. This is because a properly constructed hedge position is not as risky as a speculative position, since the futures position is always balanced with a cash market position. Thus, what the hedger loses on one "leg" of the hedge (e.g., futures) is offset by a gain on the other "leg" of the hedge (cash). It is still true, however, that the hedger must meet margin calls if the futures leg of the hedge moves adversely. However, it is possible to make arrangements with brokerage firms whereby margin is deposited in the form of treasury bills and thus some interest income may be earned on the margin deposit.

# CLOSING A POSITION

A commodity futures contract is a legally binding agreement to make or take delivery of a commodity in the future. This legal commitment may be satisfied in one of two ways. First, actual delivery of the physical commodity (physicals, sometimes called wet barrels in the case of energy futures) may be made or taken. When delivery takes place it will occur at a place specified in the futures contract as the delivery point. The goods delivered must meet minimum standards according to contract specifications, and delivery occurs during the delivery month of the contract with the specific date established by the contract. The seller is obligated to deliver proper documentation, such as warehouse receipts, certification of quality, and so on. Details vary from contract to contract and exchange to exchange. Typically, the delivery point is located physically near the exchange on which the contract is traded. However, the recent international scope of the futures markets has allowed exchanges to structure the delivery points anywhere in the world.

In commodity futures, delivery occurs less than 2% of the time. The other 98% of the time the futures obligation is satisfied by offsets. The actual amount of delivery varies from exchange to exchange and contract to contract.

If a trader buys futures (is long), an offset will be accomplished by selling the same number of futures contracts for the same delivery months that were originally purchased. The exchange allows the trader to net the two positions and thus fulfill his legal original obligation to take delivery. Of course, the trader's financial position is adjusted for the difference in price of the long and short contracts.

The offset procedure is opposite for the short, or selling, position. In order to offset his short position the trader must buy contracts at the current price on the exchange.

It is always possible to offset, even on the last trading day of the delivery month. In addition, brokerage firms are very aggressive in notifying their customers about impending delivery dates. Should a trader fail to offset and be forced to take delivery, it is always possible to get legal possession of the commodity, pay storage costs for a day or two, and sell the commodity in the cash market. Arrangements for making and taking delivery are handled by brokerage firms.

In recent years a few commodity exchanges have developed energy futures contracts that do not require the closing of a position. These contracts require a cash settlement instead of the delivery or acceptance of a physical commodity. The exchange determines the cash settlement price on the last day of trading using various cash data and/or published price information. The Brent Crude Oil futures contract on the IPE is a cash settlement contract, although it does allow for Exchange for Physicals (EFP) should the parties to the futures contract agree. The electricity futures contracts in Australia and New Zealand also use the cash settlement method. (See Table 9–1 for further information on settlement methods of various energy futures contracts.)

## Exchange of futures for physicals (EFP)

The exchange of futures for physicals, or EFP, refers to a privately negotiated transaction that involves the simultaneous execution of a futures transaction on the exchange and a cash market transaction. Every EFP, therefore, has two components: a cash component and a futures component. With respect to the cash component, EFPs allow market participants complete flexibility in terms of a trading partner, delivery location, timing, and price. With respect to the futures component, EFPs allow market participants a mechanism for obtaining futures contracts and for the pricing of such contracts through private negotiations.

The main difference between EFP and the standard delivery is that the commodity exchange's performance guarantees do not apply to the cash component of an EFP because it is a privately negotiated contract. However, there is a requirement that the physical commodity delivered under the cash component be the same as the underlying futures contract or a by-product or related commodity and that the quantity of the physical commodity delivered approximate the quantity of the futures contract. For example, firms might satisfy the cash component of an EFP for electricity futures by agreeing to deliver electricity, natural gas, heating oil, or coal.

EFPs can take several forms. The most utilized EFP is when two firms that are hedging with opposite futures contracts enter into an EFP. When the EFP is posted at the exchange, the firms use the futures contracts to liquidate their existing futures positions, thus lifting their respective hedges and terminating their contractual obligations in the futures market. Another type of EFP can be arranged where one firm liquidates an existing hedge while the other firm establishes a hedge against the cash component. Finally, an EFP can take place between two firms without existing futures contracts. In this case, the firms negotiate a cash transaction and post an EFP at the exchange to establish appropriate new futures contracts as a hedge for their respective cash market positions.

# BROKERAGE FIRMS AND COMMISSIONS

Individuals and firms that wish to trade futures contracts and are not members of the exchange must work through an intermediary, called a brokerage firm. These firms act as agents for their customers and charge fees, called commissions, on the commodity futures contracts they buy and sell for their customers. The fees are negotiated and range upward to $100 per contract. The commission covers a "round turn," which is both the purchase and eventual sale (or sale and eventual repurchase) of the contract. Fees are usually payable at the time the contract is offset.

The legal and technical term for brokerage firm is "Futures Commission Merchant," or FCM. FCMs must be registered with the National Futures Association.

There are two general types of brokerage firms. The best-known type is the general commission house. These firms trade all types of securities such as stocks and bonds, mutual funds, puts and calls, as well as futures contracts. Typically they have large research departments, and the research is made available to customers. General commission houses are like financial department stores.

The other type of firm is the specialized broker who deals exclusively in commodity futures, sometimes even specializing in specific types such as energy or financial. Because these firms are specialized they are sometimes able to provide better service and better trades to customers who are also specialized.

A brokerage firm may or may not be a member of the clearinghouse of the exchange. Clearinghouses deal only with members, known as clearing members. Nonmembers must clear through clearing members. The customer has more protection if he deals with a clearing member of the exchange.

Clearinghouses deal only with exchange clearing members and not with individual accounts. Thus, the individual customer has a financial relationship with his broker. The general commission house will have literally thousands of customers. However, the clearing corporation deals only with the brokerage firm.

The term broker is often used loosely. Technically it refers to the person on the floor of the exchange who executes trades. Often the term is used to refer to the person who represents the firm to its customers. This person is a salesman but is also called a registered representative or account executive.

When a customer places an order to buy or sell with a brokerage firm the order is immediately transmitted to the firm's broker on the trading floor of the exchange, as shown in Figure 2–1. The floor broker executes the order in the trading ring, as instructed, at the best possible price he can obtain. When the trade is completed, the result, called the "fill price," is reported back to the customer immediately. If the brokerage firm is not a member of that exchange's clearinghouse, reports of the purchase or sale are also filed with the brokerage firm's clearing member.

Brokerage firms handle buy and sell orders from all over the world. The individual trader may be located thousands of miles from the exchange on which he is trading. However, because of a highly efficient communications network operated by the exchanges and brokerage firms, traders have access to almost instantaneous information about developments on the exchanges.

# MONITORING TRADING PROCEDURES

The use of energy futures trading has brought new responsibilities, including the need to monitor trading procedures to prevent losses caused by unauthorized trading. Unauthorized trading is the buying and selling of futures and options contracts in violation of company policy.

## Tools and applications

Futures contracts may be used by the energy industry as a hedging tool, a liquid instrument used to offset the risk of adverse price swings. Crude producers can sell futures contracts to lock in profits on future production. End users can buy futures contracts rather than risk price increases. Yet the simple hedge of one hydrocarbon has evolved into a multitude of hedge combinations. Crack spreads enable a refiner to hedge the cost of refining crude oil. Cat cracker spreads allow refiners to lock in the costs of converting distillate into gasoline.

There are also fuel substitution spreads, which allow an end user to purchase the least expensive fuel alternative. There are even synthetic futures comprised of options. For example, by purchasing a call and selling a put, one can effectively be long in the futures market while generating income. And,

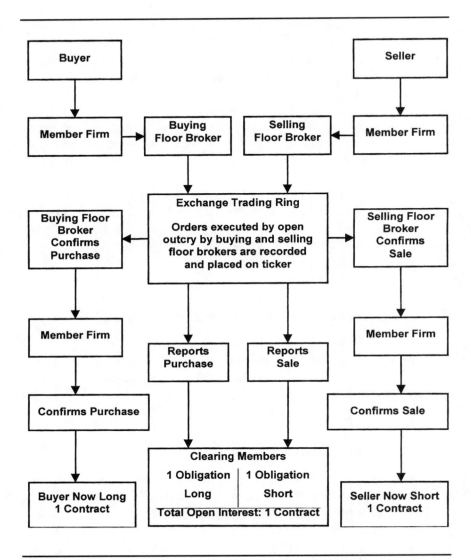

**Fig. 2–1** Initiating Trades and Order Flow for Futures and Options Contracts

most importantly, futures can be traded 84 months forward while the cash market seldom trades more than three months out.

Thus, the complexity of today's energy futures markets has made the monitoring of futures and options positions difficult. Many companies lack the monitoring procedures to evaluate the performance of hedge positions. The lack of such procedures can lead the futures trader to unknowingly execute unauthorized trades by extending himself beyond the trading boundaries conforming to company policy.

The energy industry today is more fiercely competitive than in years past. The problem of unauthorized trading is exacerbated when senior management prods traders to show profits. Successful hedging is good; the prospect of outperforming the competition in the trading profit center is, nonetheless, too sweet for many petroleum companies to resist. Numerous oil companies have established trading profit centers where traders simply speculate for profit.

When a trader incurs a small loss, however, the designs of the trading profit center may run amok. The trader tries to camouflage the loss while waiting for a compensating profit. Undetected by inadequate monitoring procedures, the loss balloons until it is too large to hide. This kind of unauthorized trading is neither premeditated nor malicious. It is encouraged by the rewards a company extends to its "good" traders and is apparently condoned since adequate controls were never implemented.

# Defensive steps

Unauthorized trading is perpetuated by mistakes that oil companies make in establishing commodity accounts and internal control systems. The three defenses against unauthorized trading are:

1. The board of directors' authorizations and directives
2. Properly established company commodity accounts
3. Documenting and monitoring futures and options trading

The board of directors must first establish that there exists a need to buy and sell energy futures and options. This decision can only be responsibly reached after reviewing information from senior management, traders, the controller, the treasurer, the internal auditor, and the futures commission merchant (FCM). Next, the board must specify the company's use of the petroleum futures market; that is, whether the company is to use the market for hedging or for trading, or both. In addition, the board must determine which individual has the authority to open commodities accounts (to prevent conflicts of interest, this should never be the trader).

The board must also establish trading and position limits. Initially low, these limits can be expanded with time and growing expertise in the use of the futures markets. Finally, the board must continually evaluate the company's use of the futures market. This requires that standards be established by which to judge performance. (It should be remembered that the standard for a successful hedge is a profit between a cash and a futures position, not positive cash flow from the futures position.)

The second defensive step in initiating a futures program is the proper filing of the corporate papers necessary to open a commodity account. There are four key forms:

- Risk disclosure statements
- Corporate authorization
- Hedge agreement
- Customer agreement form

Risk disclosure statements are mandated by the Commodity Futures Trading Commission (CFTC). By signing this form the company acknowledges the risks involved in trading futures and options.

The corporate authorization states that the company has authority from its board to trade futures and options and also names the individual(s) responsible for opening the account.

The hedge agreement specifies the futures contracts for which the company is a bona fide hedger.

The standard customer agreement form between the company and the FCM specifies each party's obligations. Generally, the brokerage firm is obligated to promptly notify the company regarding trades executed and margin calls. In turn, the company is obligated to make margin payments in a timely manner.

The standard customer agreement is often missing important data that can help prevent unauthorized trading. Additional information should be submitted to the FCM including the names and titles of the individual(s) authorized to trade and whether or not they are permitted to open their own personal commodity accounts. Note that although this will prohibit a trader from opening an account with the same FCM, it does not guard against him opening an account elsewhere. A company that does not wish to have its employees trading for their own accounts must reach agreements with them.

The company should also provide the FCM with the names of the individuals responsible for handling margin calls, and the individuals authorized to receive documentation of trading activity. The company should also set daily trading and position limits and convey these to the FCM. Although the FCM may not want to take responsibility for monitoring this information, it should at least inform company management when trading limits are exceeded.

The third and most crucial defense against unauthorized trading is the institution of internal operational and accounting controls. The key to internal control is that no one person or department should handle all aspects of a transaction. Thus, the "multiple contact" requirement between the FCM and company personnel is essential.

## Checks and balances

The multiple contact checks and balances system is illustrated in Figure 2–2. There are five key components to this system, and the FCM is the only component external to the company. The internal components are the trader, the treasurer, the controller, and the internal auditor.

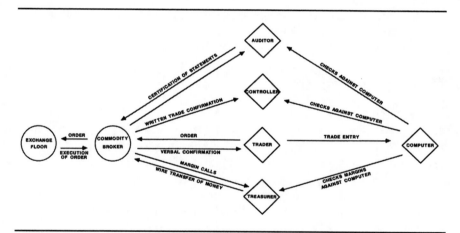

**Fig. 2–2** Trading Controls

The trader should have the right to trade the futures market, but with daily trading limits. He should be supervised by a senior official who has the authority to trade the market with expanded daily trading limits. The supervisor, in turn, reports to a hedge or trading committee. The committee, comprised of management, should evaluate hedging and/or trading positions as well as price risks associated with the company's operations.

A trade is initiated when the trader telephones the commodity broker with an order and the broker then contacts his representative on the exchange floor. Once the transaction is completed on the floor, the broker informs the trader of the order's execution and relays all the pertinent data (*i.e.*, price, quantity, and type). The trader now prepares trade entry information for the company's computer database.

The broker prepares a statement of transaction that is sent to the controller's office in the morning mail with a copy either by fax or e-mail. It is essential that the hard copy confirmation be sent in a timely manner so that if any error exists the controller can quickly call attention to the matter before the market opens. The controller's daily contact with the FCM can catch unauthorized trades promptly before prices can adversely affect the company.

The commodity broker should contact the treasury department daily, if necessary, to discuss shortages or excess margin money. The commodity broker should never discuss money transfers with the trader. Thus, if the treasurer believes that a margin call is excessive he can turn to the trader or the computer database and see whether the trader has exceeded the position limits established by the board of directors.

In turn, the treasurer, controller, and the trader are overseen by the internal auditor. The auditor should spot check trading positions and money balances during the month by requesting signed confirmations from the FCM.

# How losses occur

Unauthorized trading is a real problem for any company using the futures and options markets. The problem usually reveals itself when least expected in the form of excessive original and variation margin calls from the FCM. In one court case, a petroleum company sued an FCM for unauthorized trading, alleging that (1) the FCM was trading the account; (2) the FCM opened a personal account for the trader who was prohibited from trading his own account; and (3) the FCM allowed the trader to exceed the company's trading limits.

The jury reviewed the facts and found that the original commodity account papers filed with the FCM did not prohibit the trader from opening his own account; nor did the documents specify trading limits. The petroleum company also failed to provide multiple contacts for receiving confirmations or transferring funds. When the company admitted that it had not received many of the trading confirmations, the jury was informed that the trader, not the controller or treasurer, was the individual asked to contact the FCM and resolve the problem. Company management was kept in the dark by the trader and the result was a trading loss in excess of $8 million. Had the company implemented a proper system of internal controls, as described above, the loss would have been less than $100,000.

# TYPES OF ORDERS

When a trader asks a brokerage firm to execute a trade, the most common type of order is the "market order." With a market order the brokerage firm will execute the trade expeditiously at the current market price when the order reaches the trading floor. The floor broker will obtain the best possible price that he can. This means the lowest price in the case of a buy order and the highest price in the case of a sell order. Note that with a market order the trader does not know beforehand what price he will obtain. The price actually obtained is dependent on market conditions when the order reaches the floor and on the skill of the floor broker.

It is also possible to order the brokerage firm to execute the trade "at the open" or "at the close" in which case the floor broker will make a good-faith attempt to execute the order as close to the open or closing price as he can. In some cases the floor broker will be unable to complete the trade. This often occurs because trading is the most frantic at the open and at the close of the market, and it may not be possible for the floor broker to execute the order under such conditions.

Sometimes a trader will specify a limit price. This is called a "limit order." In these cases the trader wants to buy or sell only at a specified price or better. In the case of a "buy limit" order the price must be at the limit or lower, and in the case of a "sell limit" order the price must be at the limit or higher. This type of order has the advantage of giving the trader strict control over the price paid. The disadvantage is that the trader runs the risk of not getting the order executed at all if the broker finds it impossible to fill the order at the specified limit price or better.

Most limit orders are "day orders," which means that the order is canceled if it cannot be filled on the day it was received. It is possible to place a limit order that is in effect for a week, or a month, or is "good until canceled." In such cases the order could be executed weeks or even months after it was placed.

A "stop order" is an order that is activated once a given price, called the "stop price," is reached. It becomes a market order at that point and may be executed at a price at, above, or below the stop price. A stop order to buy becomes a market order when the contract sells at or above the stop price, and a stop order to sell becomes a market order when the contract sells at the stop price or below.

A "stop-loss" order is useful in preventing losses when prices move adversely. It is also useful in preventing large margin calls. Assume a trader buys December crude oil at $15.00 per barrel. In order to prevent heavy losses in the event that crude oil prices decrease unexpectedly, he may execute a stop-loss order, which is a stop-sell order, at $14.75. His position will be liquidated automatically if and when the market price touches $14.75 or lower. A stop-loss order to buy could be placed when the trader is short a commodity and wants to prevent a loss if prices rise. Because stop orders become market orders, the trader doesn't know at what price the trade will be executed before the fact.

# Minimum price fluctuations

Each futures contract is subject to minimum and maximum price fluctuations. The minimum price fluctuation is called a "price tick." The tick represents the smallest unit of change that may be negotiated on the floor of the exchange. For instance, one tick on a heating oil or gasoline contract on the NYMEX is .01 cent per gallon ($.0001) and every tick represents a $4.20 change in the total value of the contract. This is calculated by multiplying the minimum price change ($.0001) by the number of units in the contract, in this case 42,000 gallons. The minimum tick in crude oil is 1 cent per barrel and each tick represents a $10 change in the total value of the contract ($.01 x 1,000 barrels per contract). The minimum tick in natural gas is $.001 per MMBtu and each tick represents a $10 change ($.001 x 10,000 MMBtu per contract).

# Maximum daily price fluctuations

There is a maximum price fluctuation called "daily price limits." These limits are the maximum amount that the price of the contract can change in one day. Once the limit has been reached, up or down, transactions above or below the limit price are prohibited. For instance, if the market is up the limit, trading may occur at the limit price but not above the limit price for the rest of the day. Trading usually ceases when the limit is reached.

Daily price limits are applied to the previous day's closing price. For instance, the initial price limit move for NYMEX crude oil for the first two contract months is $7.50 per barrel, which represents a $7,500 change in the value of a 1,000 barrel contract, while the initial price limit move for the back months is $1.50 per barrel. Once the price of a crude oil contract increases or decreases by its price limit, trading may cease because no one may want to sell at limit up or buy at limit down.

Some exchanges allow for expanded price limits. If the price in either of the two nearby months of the above-mentioned NYMEX crude oil contract is limit up or limit down on a particular day, the limits may be expanded to allow for a more orderly market. NYMEX provides for a one-hour cooling-off period where the market is closed. The market then reopens with an additional $7.50 per barrel limit for the first two contract months and $7.50 per barrel limit for the back months.

Like NYMEX's crude oil contract, the two nearby trading months in NYMEX's natural gas, gasoline, heating oil and propane futures contracts also have wider daily price limits than the other trading months. The daily price limit for natural gas in the two nearby trading months is $.75 per MMBtu compared with $.15 per MMBtu in the back months, while the daily price limit for gasoline, heating oil, and propane in the nearby months is $.20 per gallon compared with $.04 per gallon in the back months.

The greatly expanded daily price limits on NYMEX contracts and the absence of price limits on IPE contracts allows the futures prices to closely follow the gyrations of the cash market.

# READING THE TABLES

Table 2–2 is an example of the headings of a futures table from a newspaper. The top line gives the name of the commodity (crude oil), the exchange on which it is traded (NYMEX, the New York Mercantile Exchange), and the size of a single contract (1,000 barrels), and the way in which prices are quoted (dollars per barrel).

---

**Crude Oil (NYM) 1,000 barrels; $ per barrel**

|      | Open  | High  | Low   | Settle | Change | Open Interest |
|------|-------|-------|-------|--------|--------|---------------|
| Jan  | 13.50 | 14.10 | 12.50 | 12.50  | −.50   | 55,000        |
| Feb  | 13.60 | 14.50 | 12.70 | 12.80  | −.50   | 120,000       |
| Mar  | 13.70 | 14.70 | 12.90 | 13.00  | −.60   | 35,000        |
| Apr  | 13.80 | 14.80 | 12.90 | 13.30  | −.60   | 12,000        |
| May  | 13.90 | 14.90 | 13.30 | 13.50  | −.70   | 8,000         |

*Volume 90,000. Total open interest 230,000 up 1,000*

---

**Table 2–2** Price Quotes for Energy Futures Contracts

The first column under the heading lists the various months for which delivery of the commodity can be obtained. For energy commodities there are 12 contracts traded for each year so that contracts expire every month and may extend out for up to 7 years in the future.

Open:       The first price of the day
High:       The highest price of the day
Low:        The lowest price of the day

These columns are left blank if a particular delivery month is not traded on a given day.

The settlement price is a concept unique to futures markets, although it corresponds roughly to the closing price in the stock market. In commodity markets the close is a period of time—usually less than two minutes—during which a large number of transactions can take place. Many traders place orders "at the close." Therefore, in commodities trading the settlement price is a representative price at which the futures contract traded during the closing period.

This representative price is estimated differently on different exchanges. Some exchanges simply average the high and low prices during the closing period. Others use more complicated estimation techniques. In general, the settlement price represents what the last price of the day would be, if there were a single price. It is the settlement price which brokerage firms use to calculate margin requirements when accounts are marked to market each day.

The change column shows the difference between the latest settlement price and the settlement price on the previous trading day.

The last column shows open interest. Open interest is the number of contracts outstanding (not yet offset) at the close of the previous trading day for each contract month. It may be thought of as the number of live contracts in existence. When a contract first begins trading, open interest is usually small. Open interest increases as the contract gets closer and closer to maturity but begins to decline as the contract nears its delivery month and hedgers and speculators close out their positions. At the expiration of the contract, open interest is always zero as all contracts are either offset or satisfied through delivery.

Volume is different from open interest. Volume represents the number of contracts that are traded each day. Speculators may trade in and out of contracts on an "intraday" basis. Thus, volume may be considerably higher than the change in open interest on any particular day.

The table can also demonstrate that the futures market for a particular commodity actually represents several contracts for different delivery months.

The focus of attention is usually on the contract that is closest to but not in the delivery month. This is called the nearby contract. Most speculative activity is concentrated in the nearby contract. Contracts other than the nearby contract are sometimes referred to as back months or deferred months.

# Behavior of Commodity Futures Prices

The conditions that exist in futures markets, perhaps more than in any other organized market, closely resemble the conditions assumed in the economic model of perfect competition. There are large numbers of buyers and sellers who compete on the basis of readily available and relatively costless information. Commodity futures contracts are homogeneous in nature and there are no significant barriers to market entry except adequate financial responsibility. Generally, there is relatively little government intervention in futures markets and exchange self-regulation is effective in preventing manipulation and unfair practices. Thus, contract prices are determined in a highly competitive environment. The result of this is that futures markets are very efficient markets.

In an efficient market, prices approximate the true value of the product being traded. Informed traders meet and operate in a competitive environment and the prices that result represent a consensus concerning the value of commodities for delivery in the future. Of course, there will often be disagreements among market participants regarding true value. It is such disagreements that cause prices to change. There will often be discrepancies between actual prices and true value, but in an efficient market actual prices will fluctuate in the area of true value.

The price of a futures contract is related most importantly to the current price of the underlying cash commodity that is deliverable on the contract. Even though actual delivery is a relatively rare occurrence, the possibility of delivery forces a close relationship between cash and futures prices. Various other factors determine the exact relationship between cash and futures prices.

The relationship between cash and futures prices is a very important one in futures markets. This relationship is labeled "basis." Because hedgers have positions in both cash and futures markets, the effectiveness of any particular hedge is dependent upon a close relationship between cash and futures prices, that is, a reasonably stable basis. An understanding of this relationship is crucial to an understanding of hedging in futures markets.

# PRINCIPLES OF FUTURES PRICES

Hedging and speculation in commodity futures markets hinge on two important principles—parallelism and convergence. Both are related to the relationship between cash and futures prices.

Parallelism occurs because the same factors that impact on cash prices tend also to impact on the price of the commodity for future delivery. In other words, there tends to be a high correlation between cash and futures prices. Traders on commodity exchanges have access to the same information as cash market traders and this information is efficiently reflected in futures prices. In addition, because commodities are storable there is always the possibility of storing commodities for delivery against the contract in the future. This gives rise to a cash-futures arbitrage mechanism that forces a close relationship between cash and futures prices.

It is the principle of parallelism of cash and futures prices that allows hedging to be effective. The basic notion of hedging is that the hedger assumes a position in the futures market that is financially opposite to his position in the cash market. Because cash and futures prices tend to move in tandem, gains and losses in the cash market are offset by losses and gains in the futures market. The result of the combination of the cash and futures positions is a reduction in the variability of the combined positions as compared with the variability of the cash position alone. Parallelism assures that there is a substantial reduction in variability because the prices of cash and futures positions vary together closely.

Although the correlation of changes in cash and futures prices has usually been found to be quite high, it is never perfect. As a result, hedges are seldom perfect. There remains some element of risk involved in hedging. However, the remaining risk tends to be quite small relative to the risk of not hedging at all.

The second principle of futures prices is that of convergence. Cash and futures prices tend to be the same or to converge at the expiration of the futures contract. As the futures contract approaches expiration it becomes a close substitute for the cash commodity because it is a contract for delivery of the cash commodity. At expiration, owning the futures contract is essentially the same as owning a contract for immediate delivery of the cash commodity. Thus, it must have the same price as the cash commodity; that is, the futures price must converge with the cash price. If this were not so, there would be an opportunity to arbitrage between cash and futures markets. (Arbitrage will be discussed later in this chapter.)

It is the close relationship between cash and futures prices, that is, parallelism and convergence, that allows speculators to use futures markets to speculate on the direction of change of cash prices. Because the futures price is tied to the cash price in the future, a speculator who is able to forecast changes in cash prices can use the leverage available in futures contracts to profit from his forecast. Of course, if his forecasts are not correct, the leverage will exact an appropriate toll in the other direction.

Speculators use various means in their attempts to forecast cash prices. These include analysis of fundamental forces that influence cash prices and the technical analysis (charting) of past cash and futures prices. If the trader expects cash prices to be higher in the future, he will anticipate this by purchasing futures contracts. If the trader expects cash prices to be lower in the future, he will sell futures contracts. In the process of anticipating future cash prices, traders contribute to the efficient pricing of futures contracts.

Figure 3–1 illustrates the two principles of futures prices. It plots the cash and December futures prices for heating oil on the NYMEX. Prices are plotted weekly for a nine month period beginning in March and ending in late November.

Notice that the large changes in the price of cash heating oil are paralleled by changes in futures prices. A large cash increase or decrease is matched by a corresponding change in futures price. Thus, a hedger in the heating oil market could depend on this relationship to hedge away most of his risk. The actual outcome of the hedge would depend on timing (*i.e.*, the relationship between cash and futures prices at the time the hedge was placed and lifted). Notice that for some brief time periods the cash price was higher than the futures price. The normal relationship was for the futures price to be above the cash price. In general, the futures price will be above the cash price prior to the winter for heating oil and prior to the spring for gasoline.

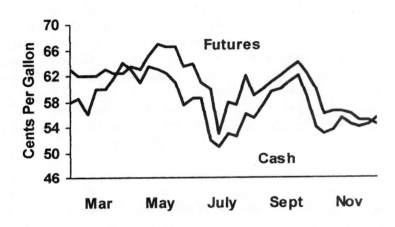

**Fig. 3-1** Cash Prices vs. December Futures

At the expiration of the futures contract the cash and futures prices converged. This is almost always true, but technical factors can cause small differences in some markets.

## STRUCTURE OF FUTURES PRICES

There is normally a difference between cash and futures prices. Notice in Figure 3–1 that the futures price is often above the cash price. When this occurs, the futures contract is said to be at a "premium" to cash. At other times, the cash price is above the futures price and the futures contract is said to sell at a "discount" to cash. This happens during periods of shortages in the cash market, which occur when the weather is especially severe and heating oil production has not caught up with demand.

Just as there is a relationship between cash and futures prices, there is a relationship between the prices of futures contracts that expire in different months. The price relationship of cash to futures contracts and the relationship between futures contracts tend to follow fairly predictable patterns which are known by the general terms "carrying charge" and "inverted" markets.

# Carrying charge markets

The normal structure of futures prices for storable commodities such as energy products is depicted in Figure 3–2. It shows the settlement prices for unleaded regular gasoline contracts on the NYMEX. The prices occurred in February and involve futures contracts for delivery of gasoline in the months of March, April, May, and June.

It is typical for gasoline futures to exhibit such a pattern during the spring months. In fact, the normal structure of futures prices is a stairstep upward

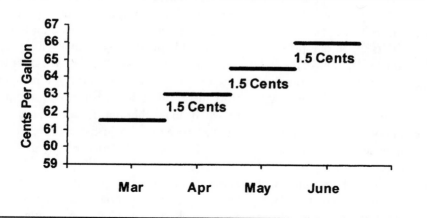

**Fig. 3-2** Contango Market, Unleaded Regular Gasoline Futures

during those time periods when there are adequate cash market supplies. This means that deferred contracts sell at a premium to nearby contracts and nearby contracts sell at a premium to cash. Another name for a premium or carrying charge market is "contango market" or just "contango."

The structure of futures prices shown in Figure 3–2 is related to the cost to carry physical commodities held as inventory. These carrying charges are comprised of storage costs, insurance costs, and interest costs on funds borrowed to purchase inventory.

Market participants who need the physical commodity in the future will choose the cheapest source of supply. This supply may come from purchasing the cash commodity and storing it or from purchasing the futures contracts and taking delivery. Because there are no carrying charges on futures contracts, other things remaining equal, the futures contract will be preferred to holding the physical commodity. This will cause the prices of the futures contracts to be bid up. An example will clarify this concept. Consider the position of a gasoline distributor who needs gasoline in one month. Suppose that current cash prices and the prices of one month futures contracts are the same, $.60 per gallon. Also assume that it would cost the refiner $.015 to finance and store a gallon of gasoline for a month. This means that if gasoline is purchased and stored for a month the total cost in one month will be $.615 per gallon. Clearly the distributor would prefer to purchase the one-month futures contract at $.60 per gallon and take delivery in one month.

Given their preferences for futures contracts over holding the physical commodity when prices are the same, holders of inventory will buy futures contracts rather than holding inventory. This will cause the demand for futures contracts and futures prices to increase. In addition, the holders of inventory may choose to sell some of the cash product or purchase less of it. This will cause the cash price to fall. At the point where the futures price is selling at a premium equal to the cost of carrying inventory there will be no further incentive to prefer futures over cash and the market will be in equilibrium. Thus, the normal or equilibrium relationship is for the futures price to be above the cash price by an amount approximately equal to carrying costs for the time period until the futures contract expires.

When the premium on the futures contract is equal to the carrying charge, the market is said to be at "full carry." Futures markets are seldom at full carry because there are advantages to holding some of the physical commodity as inventory. This is called convenience yield. Because of the convenience of holding some inventory rather than depending completely on futures markets for supplies, the normal situation is for futures to sell at a premium to cash but not at full carry.

There are three components to carrying costs: storage costs, insurance, and interest costs to finance inventory over the period during which the cash commodity is held. Of these components, the rate of interest is the most volatile. Insurance costs are minimal on a monthly basis and stable. Storage costs run about $.007 per gallon per month and are usually quite stable, although storage can sometimes be in short supply in some locations. Interest costs on loans secured by inventory are typically at the prime interest rate plus one or two percentage points on an annual basis. This means that monthly interest costs, at

12% annual interest, would be 1% per month. Because the prime rate changes often, carrying charges also change frequently. This causes changes in the spreads between cash and futures prices and changes in the spreads between the prices of futures contracts for different delivery periods.

For example, carrying charges for heating oil worth $.60 per gallon were roughly $.015 per gallon in the month of September. If the prime interest rate had been about 10% per annum at that time, at a rate of prime plus 2%, this translates into 1% per month or about $.006 per gallon if heating oil sells at $.60 per gallon. This $.006 plus $.007 per gallon per month storage and insurance costs adds up to about $.015 per month carrying costs. Note that in Figure 3–3 the spread between the September and December heating oil futures contracts which expire three months apart was about $.03 per gallon. This is below the approximately $.045 carrying charge for three months. Thus, the deferred heating oil futures contracts were selling at a premium in December but were below full carrying charges.

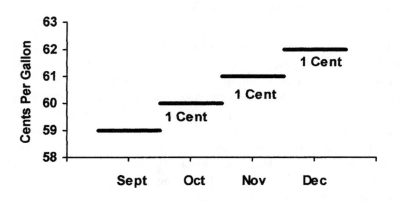

**Fig. 3-3** Heating Oil Futures

# Inverted Markets

It is not unusual in energy futures markets for cash prices to be greater than futures prices. This occurs during peak demand periods and is called "backwardation" or an "inverted market." An inverted futures market structure is illustrated in Figure 3–4. It shows the settlement prices of various heating oil contracts on the NYMEX. Futures prices form a stairstep downward. The further into the future the contract expires the greater the discount.

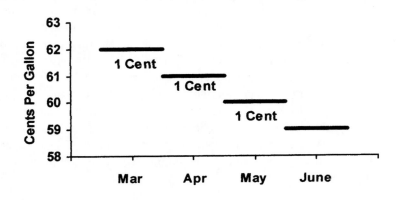

**Fig. 3-4** Inverted Market, Heating Oil Futures

Inverted markets are caused by a shortage of supply relative to demand in cash markets. The low supply and/or high demand causes cash prices to be bid upward. This encourages sales in the present rather than sales in the future. The high current cash prices signal a premium for immediate sales and thus call goods out of storage. By promising lower prices in the future the market discourages the storage of goods.

In the United States, refined petroleum products have two seasons. The gasoline or driving season lasts from April to August and the heating oil season lasts from September to March. Because the NYMEX heating oil and gasoline contracts call for delivery in New York Harbor, the seasonal demand for product and the associated price fluctuations reflect market conditions in the northeastern United States.

Petroleum futures contract prices usually depict a carrying charge pattern for contracts expiring early in the season and an inverted pattern in the later stage of the season. Thus, sometimes futures prices exhibit a pattern like the one shown in Figure 3–5. It shows the structure of unleaded regular gasoline futures prices. In this case the market is a carrying charge market during the early months of the season, but is inverted during the later months when it is expected that gasoline will be in short supply. Such a pattern occurs prior to peak demand periods when the market anticipates shortages in the cash market.

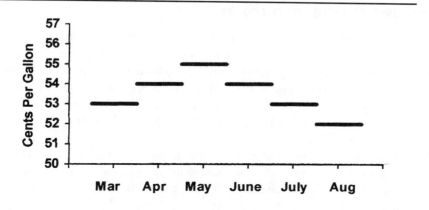

**Fig. 3-5** Unleaded Regular Gasoline Futures

The crude oil futures contract is unique in its pricing structure. During periods of substantial supply, crude oil prices are usually contango. However, during periods of a general balance between supply and demand or during periods of shortage, the market is inverted. Since NYMEX began trading crude oil futures in 1983, the pricing structure has usually been inverted. The degree to which the market is inverted depends upon the abundance of supply to demand. Because of a lack of storage for crude oil, refineries constantly need to purchase crude oil to keep operations working. Thus, refiners are usually buying for immediate consumption and putting upward pressure on spot market prices. It is this upward pressure on spot prices which causes the crude oil futures market to normally be an inverted market.

# ARBITRAGE

Many price relationships in both cash and futures markets are influenced by the arbitrage operations of market participants. The concept and theory of arbitrage is useful in analyzing the structure of cash and futures prices at different locations and at different points in time.

In economic theory, arbitrage is usually thought of as a strictly cash market phenomenon. However, many techniques in the futures markets are very similar to arbitrage and it is customary to label such transactions arbitrage.

# Cash market arbitrage

Cash market arbitrage is a riskless operation that allows traders to profit from price differences in different markets for the same commodity. The markets are normally separated geographically. The general notion of cash arbitrage is that traders purchase goods where they are cheapest and simultaneously sell them where they are more expensive. In cash markets, arbitrage opportunities occur when prices in the two markets differ by more than transportation costs between the markets.

Arbitrage can best be illustrated with the use of a simple example. Consider the market for heating oil. Assume that the full transportation cost for heating oil between New York and London is $.05 per gallon. The cost also includes insurance and other incidental expenses such as transaction costs. Given these assumptions, the cash price of heating oil in New York and London cannot differ by more than $.05 per gallon. If prices do differ by more than this there will be an opportunity for traders to profit from a riskless arbitrage of heating oil between New York and London.

Assume that heating oil is selling for $.70 per gallon in New York and $.60 per gallon in London. A trader (or arbitrageur in this case) can purchase heating oil in London for $.60 per gallon and simultaneously sell it in New York for $.70 a gallon. Of course, the trader must pay the cost of $.05 per gallon to ship the heating oil to New York, but he is still left with a $.05 per gallon profit. The key to a successful arbitrage is to be able to conduct both transactions simultaneously.

Notice that the trader purchased heating oil where it was cheapest (London) and sold it where it was most expensive (New York) and in the process heating oil flowed from London to New York. Also notice that the profit opportunity was riskless once the trader was able to lock in the prices of the two markets.

In the process of taking advantage of arbitrage opportunities, the arbitrageurs eliminate the price differences. This also eliminates the arbitrage opportunity in the two markets. Thus, each arbitrage opportunity in a commodities market contains the seeds of its own destruction because the actions of arbitrageurs quickly eliminate such opportunities.

Figure 3–6 shows the demand and supply curves for heating oil in New York and London when the prices were $.70 and $.60 per gallon, respectively. Notice that because there are separate supply and demand curves in each market there are also different prices in each market. If prices differ by more than transportation costs, market forces will cause prices to converge. In the process of taking advantage of the price difference, traders purchased heating oil in

London where it was cheapest. This caused the demand curve for heating oil in London to shift to the right as illustrated by the dashed demand curve. Thus, the actions of traders would cause the price of heating oil in London to increase above $.60 per gallon.

Traders simultaneously sold heating oil and delivered it in New York. This caused the supply curve for heating oil in New York to shift to the right as illustrated by the dashed supply curve in Figure 3–6. Thus, the price of heating oil in New York decreased.

The arbitrage process caused the New York price of heating oil to decrease and the London price of heating oil to increase. Because prices were driven closer together the opportunity to profit from arbitrage was reduced. At the point where the price difference between New York and London is less than the $.05 transportation cost, the arbitrage opportunity no longer exists and heating oil markets would be in equilibrium.

It is the arbitrage process that keeps prices in geographically dispersed markets close together. This process is greatly aided by electronic communications, which gives the trader access to nearly instantaneous information around the world. A good illustration of this is the prices of foreign currencies in foreign exchange markets. These prices are very closely related worldwide because there are a large number of traders (including large multinational banks and corporations) with access to information who are constantly alert for arbitrage opportunities to take advantage of even the smallest price divergences. This is especially efficient in the case of currencies because they can be transferred as a bookkeeping transaction and no physical goods must be transferred.

The arbitrage process also causes the prices of energy in various locations of the country and the world to bear a reasonably fixed relationship to one another. Price differences are typically related to transportation costs and prevailing product flows between markets. Price relationships between markets can change with the availability of transportation. For instance, disruptions can occur because of rail strikes and river freezings. Changes in demand patterns can also cause price relationships between markets to change. The market forces generated by market participants including arbitrageurs cause the market prices in various locations to reflect rapidly and efficiently the supply and demand conditions in different markets as well as the transportation costs between them.

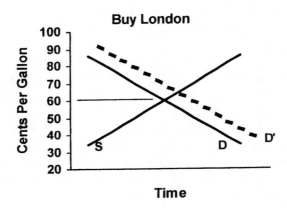

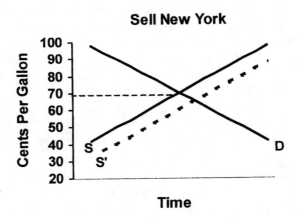

**Fig. 3-6** New York—London Price Convergence

In summary, the general notion behind arbitrage is that traders are alert to arbitrage opportunities and purchase commodities in lower-priced markets and sell them in higher-priced markets. In the process of buying low and selling high, traders cause the prices in different markets to be driven together. In other words, arbitrage causes the price spreads in different markets to be narrowed. Again, note that true arbitrage opportunities are generally riskless when they occur.

# Cash/Futures arbitrage

There is a normal tendency for futures prices to be above cash prices. This is labeled a carrying charge market and occurs because there is a cost to store and finance cash commodities but no storage or finance costs on commodities obtained in the futures market. Therefore, if the cash and futures prices were equal, users would prefer to assure their supply by buying futures contracts and taking delivery because they don't have to pay for storing the goods. This causes the demand for futures contracts relative to the cash commodity to increase, and futures prices are driven above cash prices.

The amount that the futures price can rise above the cash price is limited by arbitrage. If futures prices rise above cash prices by more than carrying charges, there will be an opportunity for traders to arbitrage the cash and futures markets. Traders will purchase the cash commodity and simultaneously sell the futures contract. They will then finance and store the cash commodity and deliver it on the futures contract. Because the futures price was above the cash price by more than carrying charges, traders will profit.

Cash futures arbitrage is similar to cash market arbitrage in that arbitrage opportunity creates market forces that narrow the differences between cash and futures prices. In the process of purchasing the cash commodity and selling futures contracts, the price in the cash market will increase and the futures price will decrease.

Suppose the cash price of heating oil is $.60 per gallon and that it costs $.015 per month to finance and store the oil. Assume further that the price of the one month futures contract is $.63 per gallon. Traders will buy cash heating oil at $.60 per gallon and simultaneously sell futures contracts for an equal number of units at $.63 per gallon. They will store the heating oil for one month at a cost of $.015 per gallon. Thus their total cost in one month is $.615 per gallon. Traders have the option of delivering the heating oil in satisfaction of the short futures contract at an effective price of $.63 per gallon or offsetting the futures contract at a profit and selling the heating oil in the cash market. These are equivalent transactions. In both cases there is a profit of $.015 per gallon.

In the previous example, traders purchased the heating oil, increasing demand in the cash market, and sold the heating oil futures contract, increasing supply. This means that the cash price would be driven upward and the futures price downward. As a result, the futures price would fall until it was less than the cash price plus carrying charges. (It is this fall in the futures price relative to the cash price that makes offsetting rather than delivery possible.) At this point there is no further incentive to arbitrage.

Futures prices rarely rise above cash prices by more than carrying charges. In addition, futures markets are seldom at "full carry." Full carry means that the futures price is above the cash price by an amount equal to carrying charges. Typically, futures markets are at less than full carry, reflecting the relative convenience to users of holding some cash commodities rather than relying exclusively on futures markets for their flow of commodities.

Arbitrage limits the amount that futures prices can rise above cash prices. The limit is the carrying charge per unit of time on the cash commodity. However, the opposite is not true. There theoretically is no limit on the amount that the futures price can fall below the cash price in an inverted market. In a practical sense, however, expiration of the futures contract and the resultant convergence of cash and futures prices limit the time and amount of inversion.

Just as there is a limit on the amount that the futures price can rise above the cash price, there is a limit on the amount that the price of a deferred futures contract can rise above a nearby futures contract price.

Assume that the price of a nearby gasoline contract is $.60 per gallon and that the price of a three-month deferred contract is $.66. Assume further that storage and finance costs are $.015 per month. Thus, a trader can buy the nearby contract and simultaneously sell the three-month deferred contract. He can then take delivery on the nearby contract at expiration, store the gasoline for three months, and deliver on the deferred contract. He would pay $.60 for the gasoline plus three months storage of $.045 for a total cost of $.645. The gasoline would be sold at $.66, a profit of $.015 a gallon.

In practice, the above transaction would probably not involve delivery and storage of any wet barrels. Rather, all transactions would take place in futures markets. As the prices between the contracts narrowed, traders would offset both contracts and pocket a profit equal to the change in the price difference between the contracts. This is called spread trading.

Because traders are alert to such possibilities, price differences between nearby and deferred contracts are seldom more than carrying costs. When such price differences do occur, the actions of traders will drive prices closer together and eliminate the arbitrage possibilities.

It is the possibility of arbitrage that causes cash and futures prices to converge at the expiration of a futures contract. Price differences at expiration would be an arbitrage opportunity. If the cash price were below the futures price, traders would buy cash product and simultaneously sell futures contracts and make delivery at the higher price, profiting by the amount of the price difference. If the futures prices were below the cash price, parties desiring the actual physical product would prefer to buy futures contracts and take delivery at the lower price.

In both cases the actions of market participants would cause prices to con-verge. As a practical matter, cash and futures prices are seldom exactly equal at expiration because of frictions, such as transaction costs, in the arbitrage process. The prices are typically close enough so that for all practical purposes they are the same.

For seasonally demanded commodities, such as heating oil and gasoline, there is a need to assure that adequate supplies of the product are stored and available for those periods of the year when the commodity is in peak demand. Futures markets are part of a very efficient allocation mechanism whereby the relationship between cash and futures prices gives signals that cause goods to be stored or consumed. This rationing process is one of the major contributions of futures markets to the smooth flow of goods from producers to ultimate consumers.

Prior to peak demand periods there is a surplus of wet barrels as refiners build inventories in anticipation of peak demand. This causes cash prices to decrease relative to futures prices. As futures prices rise relative to cash prices there is an incentive to purchase and store the cash commodity and simultane-ously sell it at a higher price in the future. This effectively hedges the price risk of carrying inventory. Thus, a carrying charge structure of futures prices causes goods to be stored for the future. In essence, the futures market pays carrying charges as the futures price rises above the cash price.

Cash prices will increase if there is a current shortage in the cash market. This will cause an inverted futures market with cash prices above futures prices. This provides a negative incentive to store goods, and goods will effectively be called out of storage for immediate consumption. As new supplies become avail-able the cash price will decrease and the market will again become a carrying charge market.

It can be seen that futures markets contribute greatly to the efficient rationing of goods over time. This rationing is accomplished solely by the mar-ket mechanism with no government intervention. Guided only by the signals provided by cash and futures prices, literally thousands of market participants acting only in self-interest provide the very important function of allocating goods over time.

# BASIS

In order to understand hedging it is necessary to understand the concept of basis. Basis may be defined as the difference between the futures price of the commodity and its cash price:

*Basis = Futures Price − Cash Price*

Normally, the first nearby contract is used in calculating basis, although it is perfectly legitimate to talk about basis for deferred contract months.

Although there is only one price for the nearby futures contract, there are many different cash prices at various locations around the country where petroleum products are traded. Thus, there is a unique basis for each location.

Conceptually, basis may be split into two components: storage basis and location basis. (There is also a third basis, product basis, which will be discussed briefly.)

## Storage basis

In order to isolate storage basis, assume at first that we are considering only the cash price at the delivery point of the contract. Thus, storage basis will consist of the difference between the futures price and the cash price at the delivery point.

If the current futures price is labeled $F$ and the cash price at the delivery point of the futures contract is labeled $Cd$, then storage basis may be defined as follows:

*Storage Basis = F − Cd*

Suppose the price of the nearby gasoline contract which is traded in New York and expires in two months is $.60 per gallon. Also assume that the cash gasoline price in New York is currently $.58 per gallon. Given these numbers, the basis in New York is $.02.

Because the futures price is above the cash price, basis is positive. In an inverted market, the cash price is greater than the futures price and storage basis would be negative.

Basis is related to the two principles of futures prices. The first principle suggests that when cash prices change, futures prices change by about the same amount. This is the same thing as saying that basis will be relatively constant when prices change. For instance, suppose some sort of information becomes public which causes the cash price of gasoline in our previous example to increase to $.65 per gallon. The first principle of futures prices would suggest that the futures prices would rise by about the same amount, to $.675. The new basis after the price change would be $.025 rather than the $.02 before the price change. Thus, the basis was relatively constant.

The second principle of futures prices is that cash and futures prices tend to converge over time and are equal at the delivery point at the expiration of the futures contract. In a premium or carrying charge market, the basis is related to carrying charges. Cash and futures prices tend to converge at a rate roughly equal to carrying charges. Because carrying charges diminish as the contract nears expiration, storage basis also diminishes as the contract nears expiration. Of course, at expiration the cash and futures prices must be the same at the delivery point. This means that storage basis must be zero at expiration.

The tendency for the basis to be relatively constant for large price changes and its tendency to narrow over time may be visualized by examining Figure 3–7. Notice that the basis is fairly wide in the early part of the year when carrying charges are large and that it narrows as the year progresses. The basis is zero at expiration.

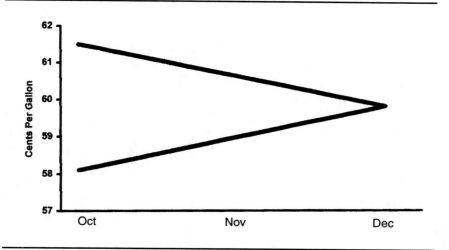

**Fig. 3-7** Convergence of Cash and Futures

The tendency for cash and futures prices to converge over time is shown pictorially in Figure 3–7. Assuming a carrying charge market, storage basis theoretically narrows at a constant rate equal to storage costs per gallon per unit of time. Of course, cash and futures prices are subject to the vagaries of supply and demand, and thus the actual storage basis and its change over time will be considerably more variable than suggested by Figure 3–7.

When the futures market is inverted the basis will also narrow as expiration nears. However, the basis is likely to be more variable because it is unrelated to carrying charges in an inverted market.

## Location basis

The differences between cash prices at various locations around the country are related to transportation costs, prevailing product flows, and the supply-and-demand situation in each local market. Arbitrage possibilities assure that the price differences at different locations bear a reasonably stable relationship to each other. Thus, one does not find heating oil or gasoline selling at widely different prices in different locations except during peak demand periods. The price of heating oil on the Gulf Coast and New York normally varies between $.01 and $.02 per gallon. However, during peak winter usage it can run as high as $.05 per gallon. Arbitrage eventually eliminates these large price differences.

Because there are different cash prices in different areas of the country, there is a basis unique to each location. The difference between the cash price at the delivery point and the cash price in a local market is called location or transportation basis. If we define $Cd$ as the cash price at the delivery point of the futures contract and $Cl$ as the cash price in a local cash market, then location basis may be defined as follows:

$$Location\ Basis = Cd - Cl$$

For instance, heating oil is usually $.02 cheaper on the Gulf Coast than in New York, but it costs about $.005 less in Philadelphia and $.01 more in Boston.

The basis at any location may be thought of as the sum of the storage and location basis:

$$Basis = Storage\ Basis + Location\ Basis$$

This is equivalent to the following:

$$Basis = (F - Cd) + (Cd - Cl)$$

Clearing the parentheses yields

$$Basis = F - Cl$$

...that was our original definition of basis. The narrowing of storage basis and the stability of location basis are depicted in Figure 3–8.

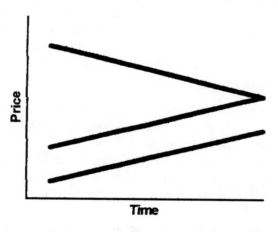

**Fig. 3-8** Convergence of Cash and Futures—Location Basis

## Product basis

The difference between the futures price and the price of a similar cash commodity is called product basis. Kerosene prices are correlated with heating oil prices. Therefore, a distributor of kerosene could use heating oil futures to hedge his kerosene price exposure. Airlines can hedge jet fuel costs by using a combination of heating oil and gasoline futures.

Residual fuel oil has a consistent price pattern with heating oil during some months and with crude oil during other months. Therefore, a user of residual fuel oil, after evaluating product basis risk, could successfully hedge his price exposure.

Thus, the prices of other petroleum products can be hedged using futures markets when consistent product basis relationships exist.

# Basis and hedging

There is a very close relationship between basis and the effectiveness of hedging. If basis does not change substantially when large cash price changes occur, then changes in cash prices experienced by hedgers will be offset by approximately equal changes in futures prices and hedgers will be effectively insulated from price risk. Systematic changes in basis related to storage costs will generate corresponding systematic profits or losses to hedgers. The reduction of storage basis over time may be to the hedger's advantage or disadvantage depending on whether he is long or short in the cash market and whether futures markets are inverted or carrying charge markets when the hedge is initiated.

# Basis changes

Figure 3–9 presents an abstract and idealized picture of changes in basis. In it, the futures price is held constant and the cash price is shown as converging from below, and thus basis narrows. In fact, due to market forces, both cash and futures prices change almost continuously because of random shocks.

Basis changes may be conceptually split into two components: systematic and unsystematic basis changes. Systematic changes in basis are also represented in Figure 3–9.

Systematic changes in basis are caused by the diminution of carrying charges over time. As the futures contract nears expiration, the cost to carry inventory until expiration decreases. In a full carrying charge market, the cash and futures prices will converge at a rate approximately equal to carrying costs per unit of time. For instance, if it costs $.015 per month to store heating oil, then in a full carry market basis will narrow by approximately $.015 per month. If the difference between cash and futures prices is not full carry, basis will still narrow over time but at a slower and less predictable rate. In an inverted market, cash and futures prices will converge at expiration, but the rate of convergence is unpredictable. In an inverted market, basis changes are unsystematic in nature.

Unsystematic changes in basis are random and unpredictable in nature. They are small and large perturbations caused by differential changes in cash and futures prices. A more realistic picture would show cash and futures prices trending upward over time and the difference between the two (basis) narrowing at a

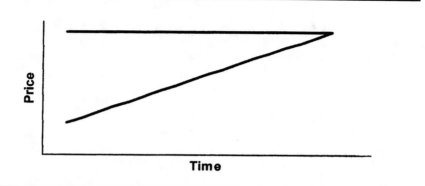

**Fig. 3-9** Convergence of Cash and Futures with Futures Held Constant

fairly constant rate with random differences superimposed. Of course, the trend in prices might just as well have been downward. Re-examination of Figure 3–1 in light of this discussion will give further insights into the nature of changes in basis.

# Speculation and Spread Trading

A large proportion of the trading activity in futures markets is conducted by speculators. Speculation may be thought of as any risky activity undertaken solely for the purpose of profit. Given this broad definition, speculation may be divided into two categories—position trading and spread trading.

Position trading consists of outright long or short positions in futures contracts. The aim of position trading is to profit from changes in the level of prices of futures contracts. Spread trading consists of both a long and a short position in different contracts of the same or related commodities. Spread trading— a technique that takes advantage of the relative price movements between futures contracts—is very similar to arbitrage. Unlike arbitrage, however, a commodity spread position is a risky position, although spreads are less risky than outright futures positions. It has been estimated that for futures markets, in general, about 25% of all trading volume is spread volume. This number is probably somewhat higher for energy futures markets.

## SPECULATION AND POSITION TRADING

All position trading is essentially similar. In the case of a long position, or purchase of a futures contract, the speculator expects the price to increase and attempts to buy at a low price and sell at a higher price. In the case of a short position, or sale of a futures contract, the speculator expects the price to fall and attempts to sell high and buy back at a lower price.

Speculators may be divided into two broad categories—inside or wholesale speculators and outside or retail speculators. Inside traders, also called locals, are members of the commodity exchanges and trade contracts for their own accounts on the floor of the exchange. They pay a small commission that includes a reduced clearing fee to the clearinghouse of the exchange. Outside or retail speculators are located off the floor of the exchange and pay higher commissions to brokers in order to participate in futures markets.

Speculation and speculators may be differentiated according to the time horizon of the speculator. Speculators may be classified as "scalpers," "day traders," and "position traders."

The scalper is an inside speculator who trades in and out of the market on a very short-term basis. If a large order to buy or sell reaches the floor of the exchange, the scalper will absorb some of the order at a small price concession and then feed the position back into the market over time. The scalper's time horizon is minutes and hours rather than days and weeks. The scalper is willing to take very small profits and losses by trading on the basis of very small price fluctuations. In the process, the scalper provides liquidity to the market. A scalper will seldom hold a futures position overnight but will close out his position at the end of each day.

A day trader holds a market position only during the course of one trading session and rarely carries a position overnight. The day trader formulates his strategy (long or short) in the morning, initiates a position, and then closes the position before trading ends.

Position traders purchase (go long) or sell (go short) futures contracts for days or even weeks at a time. They attempt to forecast and take advantage of broad price trends in the market. Successful position traders are usually well enough capitalized to sustain some losses while waiting for the predicted trend to materialize.

Most inside speculators do not limit their activity to one type of trading. The inside trader may at times be a position trader, a day trader, or a spread trader. He may also sometimes supplement his income by scalping. Exchange members may also earn commissions by acting as brokers for outside speculators and hedgers.

Inside speculators or locals are necessary for the smooth operation of the exchange. They bear risk and provide liquidity. Exchange members put up risk capital when they purchase their seats, and it may be assumed that the return on this risk capital is commensurate with the level of risk which the exchange member bears and the level of trading skill he brings to the floor of the exchange.

Outside speculators are typically position or spread traders, although increasingly the technology is available whereby outside speculators can monitor prices almost instantaneously. This allows the outside speculator to trade the market on a short-term basis. Through the use of computer technology, price information from U.S. commodity exchanges is available worldwide within seconds of trades being executed.

# Benefits of speculation

Speculation as an economic activity has sometimes been viewed with suspicion by governmental and agricultural interests. At various points in history, attempts have been made to ban "gambling contracts" or to limit speculative "excesses." Such efforts have not been totally successful because reduction or elimination of speculation in commodity futures markets usually yields results that are more undesirable than the supposed ill effects of speculation.

There are real differences between speculation and gambling. Speculators assume an already existing risk—price fluctuations in commodities. These price fluctuations would exist whether or not there were speculators to take advantage of them. Gambling, on the other hand, creates risk for its own sake, and gamblers hope to profit from the artificially created risk.

Even though speculation has often been viewed with suspicion, it has been found necessary to allow speculation in futures markets in order to generate sufficient liquidity and open interest for hedging to be effective. A futures market comprised solely or even mostly of hedgers would not be efficient enough to be useful. Hedgers in futures markets are typically "net short," which means that there are more hedgers who want to short, or sell, futures than want to buy, or be long, futures. Because there must be a long contract outstanding for every short contract, it is necessary for speculators to take up the slack.

Speculation contributes greatly to the efficient pricing of futures contracts. Ultimately, the price of a futures contract must be related to its true value—true value that is associated with the cash price and carrying charges. Speculators acting in their own self-interest cause the prices of futures contracts to be close to their true worth. In highly competitive and efficient markets, such as futures markets, the prices of futures contracts fully reflect all information relevant to present and future price formation. Any new information is rapidly reflected in both cash and futures prices. New information sometimes causes cash and futures prices to change rapidly and substantially. If it were not for the existence of speculators, hedgers might not receive a fair price for their products because the futures price could differ considerably from the true value.

# Market efficiency and the profitability of speculation

Because futures markets are efficient, it is difficult for speculators to earn a profit consistently. There are large numbers of sophisticated traders who are constantly alert for profit opportunities. There are many professional traders who analyze all available information for clues about what prices will be in the future and trade on the basis of this analysis. Because information relevant to price formation arrives randomly, cash and futures prices tend to change randomly with little lag. This has led many academic analysts to assert that futures prices follow a random walk (the "random walk hypothesis").

The general notion behind the random walk hypothesis is that financial markets, including futures markets, are efficient; that is, they closely resemble the model of perfect competition. This has been labeled the "efficient markets hypothesis." Market efficiency implies not only that prices will follow a random walk but that prices fully reflect all publicly available information relevant to price formation. In a market where prices fully reflect all publicly available information, it is very difficult to earn speculative profits.

The notion of a random walk has a very specific mathematical meaning. It suggests that at any point in time cash and futures prices are as likely to increase as they are to decrease. In other words, price changes are no more predictable than the flip of a coin.

Academic researchers and market professionals often disagree strenuously about the validity of the random walk hypothesis. Many market professionals use technical analysis in attempts to predict future price levels. As an aid in predicting the future, technicians use charts of historical cash and futures prices and believe they can identify patterns which are repetitive in nature and which are useful in predicting price changes and earning a profit. Of course, if futures prices do indeed follow a random walk, then the suggestion that prices follow repetitive patterns and that the past can predict the future is not valid. Despite the evidence of academic researchers, many market professionals do not believe in the validity of the random walk hypothesis and are willing to risk their money in using charting techniques. The debate remains unresolved.

There is some indirect evidence that supports the efficient markets hypothesis. If futures markets are indeed efficient, then it should be very difficult for all but the most astute traders to earn profits consistently by speculating in futures markets. The efficient markets hypothesis does not suggest that it is impossible to earn speculative profits consistently, only that such profits will be available only to the exceptional trader.

There is evidence that the vast majority of speculators (about 75%) consistently lose money. Other studies have found that the small or casual trader consistently loses money. The only group that consistently earns money in futures markets is the traders with large positions, presumably the most sophisticated traders. Here the evidence suggests that although such traders do earn money, their profits are not large relative to the money invested.

The volatility of futures prices combined with high leverage makes it difficult for all but the most highly capitalized to make money in futures markets. Unless the trader has sufficient capital to absorb adverse price moves, even the ability to forecast prices exactly could result in losses.

To illustrate, suppose the current price of a futures contract on commodity X, which expires in six months, is selling at $1.00 per unit. Assume further that a trader knows with certainty that the cash price of the underlying commodity at expiration in six months will be $1.50 per unit. It would seem as though the trader could not lose. However, if in the interim the futures price should decline sufficiently, the trader will receive a margin call and be required to deposit additional money. If the trader cannot meet the margin call the position will be closed out by the brokerage firm. Thus, even with a high degree of forecasting accuracy a trader must have sufficient capital in order to profit consistently in futures markets. In addition some futures contracts have had an uncanny ability to show a very sharp price dip just prior to a major price increase.

The conclusion seems to be that it is very difficult to make money consistently by taking outright positions in futures markets. This is because the prices of futures contracts are determined in a highly efficient market. Operationally, this means that new information not previously reflected in cash and futures prices probably arrives randomly and frequently and is rapidly and accurately reflected in cash and futures prices.

However, even though absolute prices follow a random walk, there is little or no evidence to suggest that the relative prices of futures contracts follow a random walk. Traders take advantage of relative price changes with spread trading.

## SPREADS

Spread trading involves taking a long position in one futures contract and simultaneously taking a short position in another, related futures contract. Thus, a spread consists of two equal and opposite futures positions.

The most important feature of a spread position is that absolute price changes are unimportant. A gain on one leg of the spread position is offset by a loss on the other leg. Only if the relative prices of the two contracts change will a profit or loss result.

A firm understanding of spread trading is essential to understanding the discussion of hedging techniques which follows. Spread positions may be initiated in futures contracts for different but related commodities, for different delivery months of the same commodity, and for the same commodity traded on different exchanges. For discussion purposes spreads involving related commodities will be utilized, but the general principles that are discovered apply to all kinds of spreads.

Assume that there are futures contracts traded for two related commodities, X and Y. The six-month futures contracts for both X and Y are selling at $1.00 per unit. Now, suppose a trader sells one contract of X and purchases one contract of Y. The spread position will neutralize price risk; any profit that arises from a decrease in the price of X will be offset by a loss on the long Y contract. For instance, suppose the prices of both X and Y fall to $.75. The chart below illustrates the initial spread position and the position at termination when the spread position is offset by purchasing the contract(s) originally sold and selling the contract(s) originally purchased.

|  | X | Y | Spread (X – Y) |
|---|---|---|---|
| Initial Position | Sell $1.00 | Buy $1.00 | $.00 |
| Terminal Position | Buy $.75 | Sell $.75 | $.00 |
|  | Gain $.25 | Loss $.25 |  |
|  | Net gain $.00 | | |

If the trader were to offset the spread by purchasing X and selling Y, the net result would have been no profit or loss on the spread position. A similar result occurs if the prices of X and Y increase by similar amounts.

If the prices of X and Y do not increase and decrease by equal amounts, then some profit or loss results. Suppose the prices of X and Y both decrease but that X decreases by more than Y, as follows:

|  | X | Y | Spread (X – Y) |
|---|---|---|---|
| Initial Position | Sell $1.00 | Buy $1.00 | $.00 |
| Terminal Position | Buy $.75 | Sell $.80 | –$.05 |
|  | Gain $.25 | Loss $.20 |  |
|  | Net gain $.05 | | |

Because the price of X fell more than the price of Y, the profit on the short X position was greater than the loss on the long Y position. Absolute price changes were neutralized and only the price difference between X and Y mattered. The net gain of $.05 was equal to the amount that the spread changed, from $.00 to $.05.

Suppose the prices of both X and Y increase but that X increases more than Y, as follows:

|  | X | Y | Spread (X – Y) |
|---|---|---|---|
| Initial Position | Sell $1.00 | Buy $1.00 | $.00 |
| Terminal Position | Buy $1.30 | Sell $1.24 | $.06 |
|  | Loss $.30 | Gain $.24 |  |
|  | Net loss $.06 | | |

It is no coincidence that the amount of profit or loss is related to the change in the spread between the two contracts. Typically, however, the initial spread between the prices of the two contracts involved is not zero. This does not change the general result that the amount of gain or loss is equal to the change in spreads.

Consider the same two commodities, X and Y, but assume that the initial price of the contract for X is $ 1.00 per unit and that the initial price of Y is $1.20 per unit. The futures contract for commodity X is sold and the futures contract for commodity Y is purchased. Also assume that the prices of X and Y both decrease but that the price of X decreases by more than the price of Y.

|  | X | Y | Spread (X – Y) |
|---|---|---|---|
| Initial Position | Sell $1.00 | Buy $1.20 | –$.20 |
| Terminal Position | Buy $.75 | Sell $1.00 | –$.25 |
|  | Gain $.25 | Loss $.20 |  |
|  | Net gain $.05 | | |

There are two things to note about the above illustration. First, as in the previous case, absolute price changes in the two contracts are neutralized by the combination of a long and short position. Second, the absolute value of the spread widened from $.20 to $.25 and there was a $.05 profit on the spread. The profit was equal to the amount that the spread widened. It might also have been the case that the spread narrowed. In this case the spread would generate a loss:

|  | X | Y | Spread (X – Y) |
|---|---|---|---|
| Initial Position | Sell $1.00 | Buy $1.20 | –$.20 |
| Terminal Position | Buy $1.10 | Sell $1.25 | –$.15 |
|  | Loss $.10 | Gain $.05 |  |
|  | | Net loss $.05 | |

Even though both contract prices increased, the spread between them narrowed by $.05 and the spread position generated a $.05 loss. If the initial positions had been reversed, that is, if Y had been sold initially instead of X, then the first profit-and-loss situation outlined above would also have been reversed:

|  | X | Y | Spread (X – Y) |
|---|---|---|---|
| Initial Position | Buy $1.00 | Sell $1.20 | –$.20 |
| Terminal Position | Sell $.75 | Buy $1.00 | –$.25 |
|  | Loss $.25 | Gain $.20 |  |
|  | | Net loss $.05 | |

The second situation, which previously generated a loss, now generates a gain:

|  | X | Y | Spread (X – Y) |
|---|---|---|---|
| Initial Position | Buy $1.00 | Sell $1.20 | –$.20 |
| Terminal Position | Sell $1.10 | Buy $1.25 | –$.15 |
|  | Gain $.10 | Loss $.05 |  |
|  | | Net gain $.05 | |

It is possible to generalize from the situations described above and to develop two general rules about spreads. If these rules are consistently applied, they allow the trader to know whether a widening or narrowing of spreads will generate a profit or loss.

**Spread Rule 1:** If the spread between two contracts narrows, a profit will occur if the lower-priced contract has been purchased and the higher-priced contract sold. A loss occurs when the spread narrows if the lower-priced contract is sold and the higher-priced contract purchased.

**Spread Rule 2:** If the spread between two contracts widens, a profit will occur if the lower-priced contract has been sold and the higher-priced contract purchased. A loss occurs when the spread widens if the lower-priced contract is purchased and the higher-priced contract sold.

A shorthand version of the rules is useful in deciding which contracts to buy and sell when the trader has some expectation about what is going to happen to the spread between two contracts:

Rule 1: If spreads are expected to narrow, buy low and sell high.

Rule 2: If spreads are expected to widen, buy high and sell low.

Suppose that the price of X is $1.75 and that the price of Y is $1.34. A trader expects that this spread will narrow. Using Rule 1 the lower-priced contract (Y) should be purchased and X should be sold in order to buy low and sell high. Profits will result if spreads do narrow regardless of what happens to the absolute prices of the contracts. Suppose that the price increases dramatically and that spreads do narrow, as follows:

|  | X | Y | Spread (X – Y) |
| --- | --- | --- | --- |
| Initial Position | Sell $1.75 | Buy $1.34 | $.41 |
| Terminal Position | Buy $2.50 | Sell $2.24 | $.26 |
|  | Loss $.75 | Gain $.90 |  |
|  | Net gain $.15 | | |

The spread between the two contracts narrowed from $.41 to $.26 and the net gain for the spread position was $.15, the exact amount that the spread narrowed. The spread position would also generate a profit if absolute prices fall as long as spreads narrow:

|  | X | Y | Spread (X – Y) |
| --- | --- | --- | --- |
| Initial Position | Sell $1.75 | Buy $1.34 | $.41 |
| Terminal Position | Buy $1.10 | Sell $1.00 | $.10 |
|  | Gain $.65 | Loss $.34 |  |
|  | Net gain $.31 | | |

If the trader expects the spread between X and Y to widen, the proper strategy is to use Rule 2 and purchase the higher-priced contract (X) and sell the lower (Y).

The spread rules almost always work if applied consistently. Occasionally it happens that the rules are apparently contradicted and do not work. This occurs only when the price relationship between the two contracts is reversed; the higher-priced contract becomes the lower and vice versa. What happens is that initially spreads change in the expected direction, but once the spread narrows to zero the price relationship is reversed. As long as the direction of relative price change continues in the same direction as was originally expected, the spread will generate a profit. Consider the following, where spreads are expected to narrow:

|  | X | Y | Spread (X – Y) |
|---|---|---|---|
| Initial Position | Buy $1.00 | Sell $1.05 | –$.05 |
| Terminal Position | Sell $.80 | Buy $.80 | $.00 |
|  | Loss $.20 | Gain $.25 |  |
|  | Net gain $.05 |  |  |

Notice that the spread narrowed by $.05 and the gain on the spread position was $.05 because the lower-priced contract (X) was purchased and the higher-priced contract (Y) was sold. However, when Y decreases so much in price that the spread narrows to zero and the price of Y goes below X, the spread then begins to widen:

|  | X | Y | Spread (X – Y) |
|---|---|---|---|
| Initial Position | Buy $1.00 | Sell $1.05 | –$.05 |
| Terminal Position | Sell $.80 | Buy $.70 | $.10 |
|  | Loss $.20 | Gain $.35 |  |
|  | Net gain $.15 |  |  |

Notice that the absolute value of the spread has widened when measured from the initial position, yet the spread made money. In order for the spread to widen, it first had to narrow to zero and then continued in the same direction so that the spread began to widen. Because the relative price change continued in the same direction, that is, X decreased by less than Y or increased by more than Y, the spread was profitable because X was purchased and Y was sold.

In general, the spread rules work. When difficulty is encountered, it will involve a change in sign (plus to minus or minus to plus) of the spread.

# TYPES OF SPREADS

## Intramarket spreads

Intramarket spreads are also called "intracommodity" or "time" spreads. These spreads involve the simultaneous purchase and sale of futures contracts on the same commodity for different delivery months.

Consider Figure 4–1. It shows the spread between the July and December heating oil contracts on the NYMEX with the December contract serving as the zero baseline. Note that the average spread between the December and July futures contracts was about $.04 from 1979 to 1998.

Spreads between futures contracts for different delivery months are

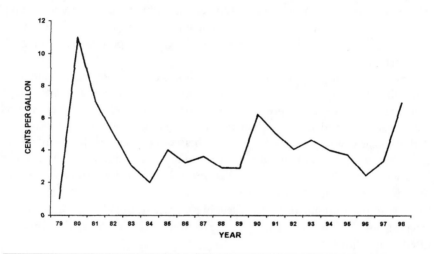

**Fig. 4–1** Price Differences Between December and July NYMEX No. 2 Heating Oil Futures Contract as of June 1

related to carrying charges. Since there are five months between July and December, and carrying charges probably averaged about $.015 per gallon, full carry between these two contracts was probably about $.075. Thus, on average, the December contract sold at less than full carry in relation to the July contract.

The reason that the December contract always sold at a premium to the July contract is that there are adequate heating oil supplies on hand in the months prior to the heating oil season. Note, however, that the July/December spread was by no means constant. It ranged from $.11 (July under December) to $.01.

These spread variations become opportunities for traders who are willing to arbitrage between cash and futures markets and for traders who want to operate solely in futures markets by trading spreads. In the case of cash/futures arbitrage, if traders think that the spread between months is too large, there will be an incentive to purchase nearby contracts, take delivery, and store the goods in order that they may be delivered on the deferred contract. If spreads between delivery months are too narrow, then some market participants will prefer to purchase futures contracts to lock up their future supply rather than pay carrying charges to store the physical commodity.

Traders who are familiar with the workings of futures markets will know which spreads between delivery months are appropriate at any point in time. Sometimes the vagaries of supply and demand cause spreads to differ from the expected spreads. In such cases, spread traders will attempt to take advantage of the situation.

Suppose that July heating oil is trading at $.60 per gallon and that December heating oil is trading at $.72 per gallon. A trader is convinced that the July/December spread is too wide. Therefore, his expectation is that spreads should narrow when the market comes back into equilibrium. If the spread trader has the courage of his convictions, he will apply Rule 1 and buy the July contract, which is the lower priced, and sell the December contract, which is the higher priced. In futures market parlance, he will buy the nearby and sell the deferred contracts. Assume the trader initiates the spread position in April and offsets in May when spreads have indeed narrowed from $.12 to $.05. The trader's position before and after the spread is lifted is as follows:

|  | July Heating Oil | December Heating Oil | Spread |
|---|---|---|---|
| Initial Position | Buy $.60 | Sell $.72 | $.12 |
| Terminal Position | Sell $.64 | Buy $.69 | $.05 |
|  | Gain $.04 | Gain $.03 |  |
|  | Net gain $.07 | | |

Notice that the spread narrowed by $.07 per gallon and that the spread was profitable by $.07 per gallon.

The above example is oversimplified because it does not take into account the number of gallons of heating oil delivered on each contract, the total value of the contract, or the margin requirements of spreads.

Each heating oil contract calls for delivery of 42,000 gallons (1,000 barrels) of heating oil. Assuming that the above trader is long and short just one contract, the above example converted to total dollar values would look like the following:

| | July Heating Oil | December Heating Oil | Spread |
|---|---|---|---|
| Initial Position | Buy 42,000 gal. @ $.60/gal. Value, $25,200 | Sell 42,000 gal. @ $.72/gal. Value, $30,240 | $.12 |
| Terminal Position | Sell 42,000 gal. @ $.64/gal. Value, $26,880 Gain = $.04 x 42,000 = $1,680 | Buy 42,000 gal. @ $.69/gal. Value, $28,980 Gain = $.03 x 42,000 = $1,260 | $.05 |
| | Net gain = $.07 x 42,000 = $2,940 | | |

Of course, the same result could have been obtained by multiplying the change in the spread by 42,000 gallons. If more than one contract is spread, then the gain or loss will be multiplied by that number.

Margin requirements on qualified spreads are considerably lower than the margin requirement on a single futures contract. This is because the spreads between futures contracts are much less volatile than absolute price levels. For instance, the total margin requirement on the above spread would be $337 while the margin requirement on one long or short heating oil contract would be $4,050.

Energy futures markets are not always contango markets; sometimes they invert. This typically occurs when there is severe weather and inadequate supplies of heating oil. Suppose that it is currently December and the March heating oil futures contract is selling at $.70 per gallon and the June contract is selling at $.67 per gallon. Thus, the market is inverted. If a trader were convinced that the market would be a premium market prior to March, then he would expect that the $.03 discount would narrow. Similar to the last example, he would apply spread Rule 1 and buy low and sell high. Thus, he would buy the deferred contract (June) and sell the nearby contract (March). Suppose the trader sells two March futures contracts and buys two June futures contracts. Further, suppose that by February the shortage of heating oil has eased and the March futures are selling at $.60 per gallon and June futures contracts are selling at $.64 per gallon. Thus, the market changed from a $.03 discount to a $.04 premium. The resultant profit/loss position would be as follows:

|  | March Heating Oil | June Heating Oil | Spread |
|---|---|---|---|
| Initial Position | Sell $.70 | Buy $.67 | $.03 |
| Terminal Position | Buy $.60 | Sell $.64 | –$.04 |
|  | Gain $.10 | Loss $.03 |  |
|  | Net gain $.07 |  |  |

Notice that in an absolute sense the spread widened. However, there was a change in sign of the spread. The total profit on the above transaction would be $5,880 which is the change in the spread ($.07) x 42,000 gallons/contract x 2 contracts. The margin requirement on the above transaction would be $674.

Interestingly, the actions of spreaders in futures markets reinforce the action of cash/futures arbitrage operations in that the profit opportunity is eliminated by traders attempting to profit from the perceived disequilibrium.

Consider the first example. In the process of buying the July contract, spreaders increase demand and drive the price of the July contract upward. By simultaneously selling the December contract, the price will be driven down. Thus, the actions of spreaders will cause July/December spreads to narrow. At the point where the spread is at a level which market participants consider to be normal, there will be no further incentive to put on a spread. Market forces insure that the prices of futures contracts for different delivery months are closely related to economic reality.

Often the terms "bull" and "bear" spreads are used in conjunction with intramarket spreads. The terms mean different things to different people. The term bull spread most often means that the trader expects the nearby contract to gain on the deferred contract. The general rule on a bull spread is to buy the nearby and sell the deferred contracts. Thus, in a carrying charge market when the nearby is selling at a discount and is expected to gain on the deferred, a bull spread would consist of buying the nearby and selling the deferred. As the nearby gains on the deferred, spreads will narrow and a profit will result, because the trader bought low and sold high. In an inverted market the nearby is expected to increase more than the deferred and spreads will widen. Thus, a bull spread in an inverted market will also consist of buying the nearby (higher-priced) contract and selling the deferred (lower-priced) contract.

A "bear spread" is when the nearby is expected to decrease relative to the deferred contract. The general rule for bear spreads is to sell the nearby and buy the deferred contracts. Thus, in a contango market, a bear spread would involve selling the nearby contract (lower price) and purchasing the deferred contract (higher price) when spreads are expected to widen (nearby decreases relative to deferred). In an inverted market, traders will buy the nearby contract (higher price) and sell the deferred contract (lower price) when spreads are expected to narrow because the deferred contract will gain on the nearby contract.

# Intermarket spreads

In futures markets there are sometimes relationships between the market prices of different contracts. Intermarket spreads involve the simultaneous purchase and sale of different but related commodities that have a reasonably stable relationship to each other. Delivery months which are bought and sold may be the same but they also may be different. Opportunities for intermarket spreads occur when the commodities being traded are substitutes for each other or there is some other relationship that causes prices to be correlated. Random disturbances in supply and demand in cash and futures markets can cause futures prices to diverge and give rise to intermarket spread opportunities.

**Henry Hub natural gas vs. Permian/WAHA Hub natural gas spread.** An example of an intermarket spread is the Henry Hub natural gas futures prices on NYMEX and the Permian/WAHA Hub (Western) natural gas futures prices on KCBOT. Figure 4–2 shows the difference between the last settlement prices for NYMEX and KCBOT natural gas futures contracts from September 1995 through September 1998. The typical spread between the contracts is around $.20 per MMBtu. Any significant divergence from this relationship may present a spread opportunity for the astute trader. The NYMEX-KCBOT intermarket spread is also known as an inter-exchange spread where each half of the spread is on a different futures exchange. (Unfortunately, the KCBOT natural gas futures market became inactive in 1999, thus making it impossible to complete this inter-exchange spread.)

**Heating oil vs. gasoline spread.** A better-known example of an intermarket spread is the heating oil/gasoline spread. It is a seasonal spread. The process of refining crude oil results in the production of both gasoline and heating oil. Although the proportions may vary somewhat, efficient production requires that both gasoline and heating oil be produced. The peak demand period for heating oil is the winter and the peak demand for gasoline is the summer. However, in the process of producing heating oil for the winter, it is also necessary for refiners to produce gasoline, even though the demand is lower in winter months. In producing gasoline for the peak summer driving months, refiners also produce and store heating oil.

Because gasoline is a more refined product than heating oil, it is more expensive to produce and thus should sell at a higher price. However, because of the countercyclical demand patterns between the two products, the price difference widens during the spring and summer and narrows during the winter. At times of peak demand, heating oil may sell for more per gallon than gasoline.

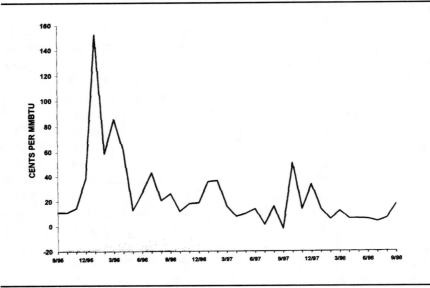

**Fig. 4–2** Intermarket Spread, Natural Gas Futures Prices, NYMEX Minus KCBOT

The changes in the difference between the prices of gasoline and heating oil give rise to spread opportunities.

In summary, this spread consists of buying heating oil futures contracts in the winter and selling gasoline futures for the same months, anticipating that heating oil consumption (demand) increases during a cold period while gasoline prices either decline or remain unchanged.

Conversely, you can buy gasoline futures in the spring and simultaneously sell heating oil, expecting that the increase in driving which warm weather brings will increase gasoline consumption. The gasoline leg of the spread should then move up faster than the heating oil.

**Crack spread.** Another important spread in energy futures is known as a "crack" spread because it mimics financially the operations of a refinery which "cracks" hydrocarbon molecules in order to convert crude oil into refined products. Such spreads are also called "paper refineries." Crack spreads are intercommodity spreads involving crude oil, heating oil, and gasoline futures contracts. Spread trading opportunities arise as price relationships among these products change.

Caution should be exercised, however, as the relationship between crude oil, heating oil, and gasoline is very complex. There are many different grades of crude oil and differences in the type of crude that can be delivered on the futures contract. Each refinery has its own cost factors which can have a bearing on price relationships. The potential spreader should carefully study contract details and underlying price relationships before committing funds to such spreads.

The notion behind a crack spread is essentially to imitate refinery operations. Refineries purchase crude oil and refine it by heating it under controlled conditions. The energy to refine the crude oil may come from the crude oil itself or from some other energy source, such as propane, which the refinery purchases.

Refining cracks the hydrocarbon atoms of the crude oil and results in a range of petroleum products. When refined, a barrel of crude oil yields 60 to 65% gasoline and gasoline-related products such as aviation fuel, ethane, propane, and other liquefied gases. The remaining part of the crude barrel yields heating oil and related products such as residual fuel oil and tar (Fig. 4–3).

Thus, approximately two-thirds of a crude barrel produces gasoline-related products, the other third heating oil and related products. Different refineries may produce different mixes of refined product from exactly the same crude oil. Some refineries may get 65% gasoline and 35% heating oil from a barrel of crude; others may get 75% gasoline and 25% heating oil.

Because refineries purchase crude oil and sell refined products in relatively fixed proportions, the prices of crude oil, heating oil, and gasoline tend to move in a parallel fashion. However, prices of each commodity also respond to factors unique to it. As prices diverge, cash market participants act to bring them back in line. It is these adjustments that give rise to the opportunity to spread futures contracts in a crack spread.

When prices of refined products rise substantially above crude prices, there exists an incentive to purchase crude oil and sell refined products. This would cause the price spread between crude and refined products to narrow. When prices of refined products fall relative to the price of crude oil, the incentive is to purchase less crude oil and run the refinery at less than full capacity. This, of course, would cause the price spread between crude and refined products to rise.

Refinery operation can be imitated in the futures market with a crack spread by buying crude oil and selling gasoline and heating oil futures. A crack spread position would be assumed when refined product prices are high relative to crude oil prices and are expected to fall. A "reverse crack spread" would involve selling crude oil and buying gasoline and heating oil futures. This position would be assumed when refined product prices are low relative to crude oil prices and are expected to rise in the future.

The smallest common denominator for crack spreads would be to buy three crude contracts and to sell two gasoline contracts and one heating oil contract. NYMEX reduces the margin requirements for intermarket crack spreads.

To imitate actual refining situations, the gasoline and heating oil contracts should be sold for delivery one month after the expiration of the crude oil contract, because refining operations take about one month.

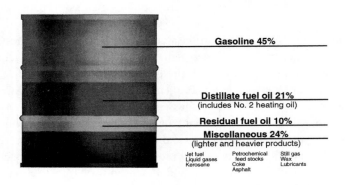

Gasoline 45%

Distillate fuel oil 21%
(includes No. 2 heating oil)

Residual fuel oil 10%

Miscellaneous 24%
(lighter and heavier products)

| Jet fuel | Petrochemical | Still gas |
| Liquid gases | feed stocks | Wax |
| Kerosene | Coke | Lubricants |
| | Asphalt | |

**Fig. 4–3** Breaking Down the Barrel (approximate petroleum product yields)

Figure 4–4 shows that in October, crude oil was priced at $18 per barrel on a 1,000 barrel contract. Assuming the proper proportion of crude oil to refined products, the three crude oil contracts had a total value of $54,000. At the same time, gasoline for November delivery was priced at $.52 per gallon and the November heating oil futures were at $.55 per gallon. Each of these contracts calls for delivery of 42,000 gallons (1,000 barrels). That gave the gasoline and heating oil contracts a total value of $66,780. This represents about a $.10 per gallon premium over the value of the crude oil. This premium covers the cost to process the crude oil, refinery margins, and probably some transportation costs. This premium is assumed to be an acceptable benchmark number.

This benchmark can be converted into a per barrel figure. Gasoline at $.52 per gallon is equivalent to $21.84 per barrel, and heating oil at $.55 per gallon is equivalent to $23.10 per barrel, because there are 42 gallons in a barrel. This represents an average of about $4.26 per barrel premium of refined product over crude oil. The difference in price between the cost of the crude oil and the price of products is called the netback. At this netback, refineries are typically at a profitable level depending upon the value of the refined products. Most refineries are quite profitable at any netback above $4 per barrel and lose money below about $3 per barrel. Over the last few years, the premium of refined product over crude has ranged from just over $1 to almost $5 per barrel.

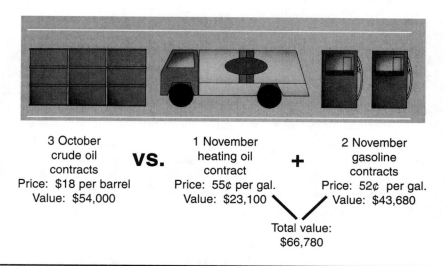

| 3 October | | 1 November | | 2 November |
| --- | --- | --- | --- | --- |
| crude oil | **VS.** | heating oil | **+** | gasoline |
| contracts | | contract | | contracts |
| Price: $18 per barrel | | Price: 55¢ per gal. | | Price: 52¢ per gal. |
| Value: $54,000 | | Value: $23,100 | | Value: $43,680 |

Total value:
$66,780

**Fig. 4–4**  How the "Paper Refinery" Works

Because gasoline and heating oil prices respond to factors other than refinery costs and margins, it is usual for the premium value of heating oil and gasoline over crude oil to change substantially as relative prices change. When the combined value of gasoline and heating oil rises significantly above the normal $4 per barrel premium, it is expected that this spread will eventually narrow. A crack spread position should be initiated where the trader purchases crude futures (lower price) and sells heating oil and gasoline futures. If the value of heating oil and gasoline should fall significantly below $3 per barrel, a reverse crack spread position should be assumed, and crude oil futures should be sold and heating oil and gasoline should be purchased.

Divergences from the normal relationship are caused by differing supply and demand uncertainties in different markets. Because of seasonal factors, gasoline and heating oil futures sometimes invert. In addition, crude oil prices are likely to anticipate political factors such as OPEC pricing decisions as well as changes in spot market conditions.

Rather than crack spread three crude oil to two gasoline and one heating oil, some refiners are fine tuning their ratios to imitate exactly their refining capabilities. It is not uncommon to see 10-7-3 ratios and 2-1-1 ratio being traded.

**Spark spread.** The newest intermarket spread is the spark spread which involves the simultaneous purchase of natural gas futures and the sale of electric futures. The spark spread offers utilities, generators, marketers, and market makers the ability to lock in a margin on current and future generation. Like a crack spread, a spark spread is a ratio which reflects the generation costs of electricity for a specific facility. The most common ratios are four electric contracts to three natural gas contracts and five electric contracts to three natural gas contracts.

**Heating oil vs. gas oil spread.** In another type of intermarket spread, similar to arbitrage, the trader attempts to take advantage of price differences in futures contracts for the same commodity traded on different futures exchanges. One such intermarket spread opportunity occurs because heating oil is traded on both the NYMEX and the International Petroleum Exchange (IPE).

In intermarket spreads the trader must be careful to analyze price differences on different exchanges. For example, differing supply and demand conditions in the United States and Europe may drive prices apart. Contract specifications are a major consideration with this type of spread. The IPE contract is for 100 metric tons of gas oil. The NYMEX contract is for 1,000 U.S. barrels, or 42,000 U.S. gallons, of No. 2 heating oil. Although both contracts are quoted in U.S. dollars, the IPE contract must be converted from metric tons, deliverable in the Amsterdam, Rotterdam, Antwerp area, to U.S. gallons deliverable in New York Harbor.

After accounting for differences in contract specifications for temperature and density, the IPE 100 metric tons contract converts to 746 U.S. barrels. At 42 U.S. gallons per U.S. barrel, one metric ton converts to 313.32 gallons. Thus, the 100 ton contract converts to 31,332 gallons. In addition, slight variations in contract quality specifications must be considered.

Combining all this information, one can convert the dollars per metric ton price in London on the IPE to a comparable dollars per gallon figure in the United States. The formula is:

$$\frac{\text{IPE \$ per metric ton}}{313.32}$$

Spread traders should also examine closely the relationship and degree of correlation between futures prices at the NYMEX and IPE. The spread between the closing per-gallon prices for the nearby contracts has averaged between $.01 and $.02 (NYMEX – IPE) for the past few years. However, the spread has been quite variable and one should consider factors such as excess European refinery capacity, weather conditions, and values of European currencies relative to the value of the dollar. Because prevailing products flow from Europe to the United States, an export license fee, which is required to ship product from the United States to Europe, accounts for the remaining NYMEX premium.

The general notion behind this spread is the same as with other spreads. If the NYMEX price should rise substantially above the normal premium, then the expectation is that this premium will eventually narrow. The proper strategy is to buy contracts on the IPE and sell on the NYMEX.

Another factor related to contract specifications is position balance. Proper spread positions require that the total value of goods contracted for in the two markets be equal. Because the IPE and NYMEX contracts are for different amounts of product, the total value of each contract is different. In order to balance positions, one should buy or sell roughly five NYMEX contracts for every seven IPE contracts. An adequate balance may be obtained with three NYMEX contracts and four IPE contracts.

For instance, suppose gas oil is selling at $130 per metric ton and heating oil is selling at $.45 per gallon in the United States. The IPE price is equivalent to $130 ÷ 313.32 = $.4149 per gallon. If the trader were convinced that the approximately $.03 per gallon spread was too high, he would want to buy seven IPE contracts and sell five NYMEX contracts. The total IPE position would be worth seven contracts multiplied by $.4149 per gallon by 31,332 gallons per contract, or $91,000. The five NYMEX contracts would be worth five multiplied by $.45 times 42,000 gallons, which equals $94,500. Thus, the total dollar amounts of the two positions are similar, though they are not perfectly balanced.

If the two markets converge, a profit will result. Suppose the IPE price falls to $120 per metric ton ($.3830 per gallon) and the NYMEX price falls to $.41 per gallon. The IPE position would be worth $84,000, which is a loss of $7,000. However, the NYMEX short position would be worth $86,100, which is a profit of $8,400. The net gain would be $1,400.

A small portion of the profit was caused by the unbalanced positions. The seven IPE contracts are for 219,324 gallons total and the five NYMEX contracts are for 210,000 gallons total. The 9,324 gallon difference causes the trader to gain when the IPE contract rises faster, or falls slower, than the NYMEX contract. The opposite is true when the IPE contract is sold and the NYMEX is purchased.

**NYMEX vs. IPE crude oil spread.** Another important intermarket spread is between NYMEX's light, sweet crude oil and IPE's Brent crude oil. Although the IPE's crude oil contract has a cash settlement mechanism rather than a physical delivery, oil traders use the spread on a regular basis to protect crude oil cargoes destined for the United States.

**Frac spread.** A fractionation ("frac") spread is an intermarket spread between natural gas futures and propane futures. Since 50% of the world's propane is extracted from natural gas, it would be prudent for a natural gas processor to manage his price risk by selling propane futures and buying natural gas futures. Just as crack spreads are quoted in dollars per barrel, terms familiar to refiners, the frac spread must be quoted in dollars per MMBtu since heating value units are familiar to most manufacturers of propane that use natural gas as a supply source. Propane in a gaseous state contains approximately 91,500 Btus. By dividing the price of propane by .0915, the manufacturer can convert to dollars per MMBtu. Thus, if propane is $.30 per gallon, its frac value would be $3.28 per MMBtu. If natural gas futures are trading at $2.20 per MMBtu, the frac spread would have a margin of $1.08 per MMBtu. Although this is a simplified example of the frac spread, manufacturers can fine-tune the spread by position balancing.

Spreads, or straddles, whether they are bull, bear, intermarket, intramarket, or inter-exchange, take on a new meaning when used in the energy futures complex. With a choice of 11 active energy futures contracts, both the novice speculator and the oil energy expert have a variety of spreading opportunities available to them. One futures contract with 10 active trading months offers 90 spread combinations—45 bull spreads and 45 bear spreads.

Extending the number of spread combinations to the thirteen contracts in the present energy futures complex, considering both intermarket and intramarket spreads, thousands of spreads are possible. It should be noted, of course, that not all energy futures contracts provide sufficient depth and liquidity in all trading months. Still, the number of spreads available with the 13 contracts is probably greater than for other futures complexes, whether agricultural, metal, financial, or stock index.

In addition, spreads provide greater leverage than outright positions because of reduced margin deposits. Thus, the use of spreads can give the speculator or hedger additional trading opportunities with reduced margin deposits.

# Hedging

The economic purpose of futures markets is to provide an arena for transferring risk among market participants. Hedgers are motivated to lay off risk in futures markets. Speculators seek risk in order to profit from it. Hedging is typically viewed as socially desirable. Speculation is often viewed as socially undesirable even though speculators contribute to the efficient pricing of futures contracts.

Because of arbitrage and speculation, the prices of futures contracts and the relationship between cash and futures prices are determined in a highly competitive and efficient market. The relationship between cash and futures prices is especially important for an understanding of hedging. The difference between futures and cash prices is known as basis.

There are two principles of futures prices and both impact on basis. The first principle is the principle of parallelism—changes in cash and futures prices tend to be highly correlated. When cash and futures prices are highly correlated, basis will be reasonably stable. The second principle of futures prices is the principle of convergence—cash and futures prices are the same (converge) at the expiration of the futures contract. This means that basis must be zero at expiration at the delivery point of the futures contract.

A hedge consists of two equal and opposite positions, one in the cash and the other in the futures market. The hedger assumes a commodity futures position (long or short futures contracts) that is opposite to the risky position that he has in the cash market (short or long cash). The resultant combination of cash and futures positions causes the hedger's risk exposure to be reduced or eliminated. Because cash and futures prices are closely related, changes in the value of the cash position are largely or completely offset by changes in the value of the futures position.

This view of hedging is correct but oversimplistic. For instance, the above view suggests that the sole motivation for hedging is to reduce risk. Although it is certainly true that one motivation is risk reduction, it is also true that many business firms attempt to use futures markets to enhance profitability. This is not to say that firms take speculative positions in futures contracts. Rather, they apply hedging techniques in such a way as to enhance profits at the same time that risk is reduced. This is often achieved by taking advantage of favorable changes in basis.

This chapter covers this expanded and more complicated view of hedging. First, different types of cash market positions are discussed. Next, the simplest case where basis is zero or constant is discussed. This is called a perfect hedge. In a perfect hedge all price risk is eliminated because of the assumption that there are no systematic or unsystematic changes in basis. This is the least realistic kind of hedging but the easiest to understand. Following the discussion of a perfect hedge the impact of unsystematic changes in basis on the hedger's position is discussed. This type of hedging reduces rather than eliminates risk and represents a more realistic view of hedging. Next the impact of systematic changes in basis is discussed. Because of the systematic tendency of basis to narrow over time, some types of hedges produce an automatic profit and others produce a loss.

When basis changes produce predictable profits, hedgers are able to use futures markets to cover part or all of their carrying costs. This is the concept of arbitrage hedging. Sometimes hedgers will choose to hedge only when they think it is to their advantage. This is the concept of selective hedging. Finally some caveats about hedging are noted and cross-hedging is discussed.

## LONG AND SHORT CASH POSITIONS

A common factor among all hedgers is that they are subject to price risk in the cash market; that is, their wealth position or their potential wealth position is impacted by a change in the market prices of cash commodities. The impact may be through variability of current inventory values or through variability of profit margins or other factors. Hedgers seek to reduce or eliminate the impact of changes in cash prices on their wealth positions.

Cash positions may be subdivided into two categories—long and short. When a hedger has an unhedged long cash position, he will suffer a decrease in wealth when cash prices decrease and an increase in wealth when cash prices increase. With a short cash position, wealth increases when prices decrease and vice versa.

Product held as inventory is a long cash position. Examples of long cash positions are gasoline marketers who have purchased gasoline from suppliers and oil companies that have purchased tankers of crude oil. In both instances, if prices decrease between the time that the wet barrels are purchased and the time they are sold, the holder will suffer a decrease in wealth.

Short cash positions involve a commitment at a fixed price prior to fixing the price of supplies. Suppose a heating oil distributor agrees to deliver product to the local school district at a fixed price for the whole season. If the distributor has insufficient wet barrels in inventory, he has a short cash position. If his cost of product increases then his profit margin will be reduced. If prices decrease then his profit margin will increase.

The ability to offer fixed-price contracts greatly enhances the competitiveness of the offerer. Futures markets offer a way to lay off this price risk. Indeed, the distributor may offer to fix the price of the contract based on the prices of futures contracts that exist at the time the contract is made.

## PERFECT HEDGING: RISK ELIMINATION

Some of the popular literature about hedging suggests that all price risk may be eliminated using futures markets. This is perfect hedging and, although a perfect hedge is possible, it is rare in practice. It is also common to suggest that when all risk is not eliminated hedges are always profitable. This is also not the case.

An important fact about perfect hedging, indeed most hedging, is that the hedger reduces or eliminates all price fluctuations, even those which might have increased his profits had he not hedged. When hedging, the hedger foregoes the possibility of a favorable price change in order that he may also reduce or eliminate the possibility of an unfavorable price change.

There are basically two kinds of hedges—the short hedge and the long hedge.

In a short hedge, also known as a seller's hedge, the hedger is long in the cash market and short in the futures market. In a long hedge, also known as a buyer's hedge, the hedger is short in the cash market and long in the futures market.

# Seller's hedge

The seller's hedge or short hedge occurs when the hedger has a long position in the spot or cash market and goes short (sells) contracts in the futures market. Short hedges are useful in reducing the variability of commodity prices held in inventory.

Suppose a trading company buys a tanker of sweet crude oil for $16.00 per barrel, delivered to the United States Gulf Coast. The cargo contains 600,000 barrels of crude and it takes about a week for the cargo to reach its destination. The purchase is made on June 1 and costs a total of $9.6 million.

The trading company is subject to price risk between the time it buys the crude oil and the time the tanker reaches the United States where the cargo is sold at prevailing cash prices. In order to hedge this price risk, the trading company will sell crude oil futures contracts which are traded on the NYMEX. Since the cargo contains 600,000 barrels and each futures contract calls for delivery of 1,000 barrels of crude oil, the trading company will sell 600 futures contracts.

Assume that on June 1 crude oil futures contracts for delivery in July are selling at $16.30 per barrel. This means that the trader's basis is $.30 per barrel because the futures price ($16.30) less the cash price ($16.00) is $.30. Once the crude oil futures contracts are sold the trading company has the following situation:

| Date | Cash | Futures | Basis |
|------|------|---------|-------|
| 6/1 | Long 600,000 barrels @ $16.00/barrel | Sell 600,000 barrels (600 contracts) @ $16.30/barrel | $.30 |

Assume that subsequent to purchasing the cargo crude prices soften and the trading company is able to sell its cargo at only $15.50 per barrel when it reaches the Gulf Coast. Assume further that the price of the futures contract moves in parallel fashion with the cash price so that basis is constant at $.30 per barrel. Thus, the futures position will be liquidated (offset), at $15.80 per barrel, at the same time that the cargo is sold in the cash market. Because the price per barrel of the futures position changed by exactly the same amount as the price per barrel of the cash position, the cargo was hedged in the futures market and there was no net effect on the trader's position. This is illustrated by the following:

| Date | Cash | Futures | Basis |
|------|------|---------|-------|
| 6/1 | Long 600,000 barrels @ $16.00/barrel | Sell 600,000 barrels (600 contracts) @ $16.30/barrel | $.30 |
| 6/7 | Sell 600,000 barrels @ $15.50/barrel | Buy 600,000 barrels (offset) @ $15.80/barrel | $.30 |
| | Loss on cash = $.50 x 600,000 = −$300,000 | Gain on futures = $.50 x 600,000 = +$300,000 | |

Net effect of the hedge
−$300,000 + $300,000 = $0

The loss in the cash market that resulted from a decrease in prices was offset by an increase in the value of the short futures position. In this case it was to the hedger's advantage to have hedged because the futures position generated a gain which offset the loss in the cash market. However, it is very difficult to predict price changes. If cash prices had increased, the cash position would be sold at a higher price but the futures position would generate a loss. Suppose that the cash price of crude increased to $16.40 per barrel and that the futures price increased by the same amount to $16.70 per barrel. The net effect of the hedge would be as follows:

| Date | Cash | Futures | Basis |
|------|------|---------|-------|
| 6/1 | Long 600,000 barrels @ $16.00/barrel | Sell 600,000 barrels (600 contracts) @ $16.30/barrel | $.30 |
| 6/7 | Sell 600,000 barrels @ $16.40/barrel | Buy 600,000 barrels (offset) @ $16.70/barrel | $.30 |
| | Gain on cash = $.40 x 600,000 = +$240,000 | Loss on futures = $.40 x 600,000 = −$240,000 | |

Net effect of the hedge
+$240,000 − $240,000 = $0

This illustrates the point that in order to gain the benefits of hedging away price risk the hedger must forego the possibility of a favorable price change in order to eliminate the possibility of unfavorable change.

The perfect hedge illustrated above depended on the assumption that futures prices moved exactly in tandem with cash prices. This is not too heroic an assumption given the short time period involved in the previous example, although it will very seldom be precisely true that futures prices change by exactly the same amount as cash prices.

# Buyer's hedge

The buyer's hedge is essentially opposite to the seller's hedge. The hedger is short in the cash market and purchases futures contracts in order to hedge the price risk. Suppose that in order to attract new customers a marketer offers to fix the price at which he will deliver natural gas to his customers in one month. However, the marketer is unable to fix his cost from his supplier until the natural gas is delivered.

Suppose that it is currently March 1 and the marketer agrees to deliver 10,000 MMBtu to his customer on April 1. In practice, marketers will sign contracts to deliver natural gas for many months into the future and will hedge in several different contracts for delivery in different time periods. For simplicity, this hedging concept is illustrated using only one month.

Assume that the current cash price of natural gas is $2.40 per MMBtu and the marketer quotes this price plus a normal margin. In order to hedge the risk that prices will increase and squeeze profits, the marketer will buy one natural gas futures contract on the NYMEX for delivery in May. Suppose the May futures contract is selling at $2.50 per MMBtu when he sells the natural gas at $2.40 per MMBtu. His initial position will be as follows:

| Date | Cash | Futures | Basis |
|------|------|---------|-------|
| 3/1 | Short 10,000 MMBtu @ $2.40/MMBtu | Buy 10,000 MMBtu (1 contract) @ $2.50/MMBtu | $.10 |

Suppose that natural gas prices firm and that by the time the marketer purchases natural gas from his supplier on April 1 the cash price is $2.60 per MMBtu. Assume that the futures price also increases by $.20 to $2.70 per MMBtu. The marketer will sell (offset) the futures contract at the time he purchases the natural gas from his supplier. The net result of the hedge will be as follows:

| Date | Cash | Futures | Basis |
|------|------|---------|-------|
| 3/1 | Short 10,000 MMBtu @ $2.40/MMBtu | Buy 10,000 MMBtu (1 contract) @ $2.50/MMBtu | $.10 |
| 4/1 | Buy 10,000 MMBtu @ $2.60/MMBtu | Sell 10,000 MMBtu (offset) @ $2.70/MMBtu | $.10 |
| | Loss on cash = $.20 x 10,000 = –$2,000 | Gain on futures = $.20 x 10,000 = +$2,000 | |

Net effect of the hedge
–$2,000 + $2,000 = $0

The loss in the cash market that resulted because of the increase in prices was exactly offset by the gain in the futures market under the assumption that cash and futures prices moved exactly parallel. Similar to the short-hedge position, any price change that generated a profit on the cash side of the hedge would generate a loss on the futures side.

A crucial assumption in both examples is that the relationship between the cash price in the local market and the futures price did not change. In both cases the cash and futures prices were assumed to increase or decrease by equal amounts and the basis remained steady. As long as this is the case it does not matter what happens to the product prices because losses in one market will be offset by gains in the other market, and vice versa.

# IMPERFECT HEDGING

When cash and futures prices do not move exactly in tandem, the hedge will generate a profit or a loss depending on relative price changes. For instance, in the first example, which involved a seller's hedge, assume that instead of a constant basis of $.30, it narrows to $.25 per barrel. The hedge will generate a profit equal to $.05 per barrel for a total of $30,000 ($.05 x 600,000 barrels) as follows:

| Date | Cash | Futures | Basis |
|------|------|---------|-------|
| 6/1 | Long 600,000 barrels @ $16.00/barrel | Sell 600,000 barrels (600 contracts) @ $16.30/barrel | $.30 |
| 6/7 | Sell 600,000 barrels @ $15.50/barrel | Buy 600,000 barrels (offset) @ $15.75/barrel | $.25 |
| | Loss on cash = $.50 x 600,000 = –$300,000 | Gain on futures = $.55 x 600,000 = +$330,000 | |

Net effect of the hedge
–$300,000 + $330,000 = $30,000

The price of the futures contract fell by more than cash prices and the basis narrowed by $.05. This caused the hedge to generate a profit of $.05 per barrel. Of course, if the basis had widened, then the hedge would have generated a loss by the amount that it widened multiplied by 600,000 barrels.

In the second example, which involved a buyer's hedge, a narrowing of the basis would generate a loss and a widening of the basis would generate a profit.

Assume that the basis narrows by $.05 per MMBtu. The hedge would generate a loss of $.05 x 10,000 MMBtu, or $500, as follows:

| Date | Cash | Futures | Basis |
|------|------|---------|-------|
| 3/1 | Short 10,000 MMBtu @ $2.40/MMBtu | Buy 10,000 MMBtu (1 contract) @ $2.50/MMBtu | $.10 |
| 4/1 | Buy 10,000 MMBtu @ $2.60/MMBtu | Sell 10,000 MMBtu (offset) @ $2.65/MMBtu | $.05 |

Loss on cash = $.20 x
10,000 = –$2,000

Gain on futures = $.15 x
10,000 = +$1,500

Net effect of the hedge
–$2,000 + $1,500 = –$500

If the basis had widened the hedge would have generated a gain.

Profits and losses on hedges are subject to the same systematic analysis as spreads, and the same rules apply. When spreads narrow, spreads generate profits when the spreader is long the lower-priced leg of the spread and short the higher-priced leg of the spread. The only difference between a hedge and a spread is that one leg of a hedge is a cash position. Thus, in a carrying charge market where cash prices are lower than futures prices, short hedgers are long cash (lower price) and short futures (higher price). When the basis narrows, short hedgers profit from the narrowing in a carrying charge market.

These effects are summarized as follows:

**Carrying Charge Futures Market**
**(Cash prices below futures prices)**
**(Contango)**

| Basis | Short Hedge | Long Hedge |
|-------|-------------|------------|
| Narrows | Profit | Loss |
| Widens | Loss | Profit |

**Inverted Futures Market**
**(Cash prices above futures prices)**
**(Backwardation)**

| Basis | Short Hedge | Long Hedge |
|-------|-------------|------------|
| Narrows | Loss | Profit |
| Widens | Profit | Loss |

In a carrying charge market, short hedgers gain and long hedgers lose when basis narrows. The opposite occurs when basis widens. In an inverted market, long hedgers gain and short hedgers lose when basis narrows. The opposite occurs when basis widens.

The change in basis which is associated with the convergence of cash and futures prices may be thought of as a systematic change. It is systematic in the sense that it is predictable and always produces a narrowing of basis. Other changes in basis are random and are known as unsystematic changes. By their nature, unsystematic changes in basis are unpredictable and are as likely to produce a narrowing of basis as they are to produce a widening.

## ARBITRAGE HEDGING

Not all changes in basis are random and unpredictable. The tendency of basis to narrow over time at a fairly predictable rate gives rise to an opportunity for some hedgers to profit consistently. This is called arbitrage hedging.

In a full carrying charge market, basis will narrow over time at a rate approximately equal to storage costs per unit of time. At less than full carry, basis will still narrow but at a slower rate. In an inverted market, cash and futures prices will converge at expiration, but the rate of convergence is unpredictable.

In a carrying charge market, which is most common for agricultural and industrial commodities, short hedgers consistently gain as basis narrows over time and long hedgers consistently lose. In a carrying charge market, short hedgers are long cash (lower price) and short futures (higher price). Short hedgers profit as basis narrows. Thus, there is a real incentive for individuals or firms with an inventory position to hedge in futures markets. The effect is for the futures market to pay all or part of storage costs. Basis gains over time will be related to storage costs. On the other hand, in an inverted market, short hedgers will consistently lose money as cash and futures prices converge. However, short hedgers may still hedge in inverted markets, choosing to pay the price of a narrowing basis as a sort of insurance premium against a large change in cash prices.

Long hedgers consistently lose money in a carrying charge market. In a carrying charge market, long hedgers are short cash (lower price) and long futures (higher price). As basis narrows because of convergence, long hedgers lose money. Thus, there is a disincentive for individuals or firms with short cash positions to hedge in futures markets. Often, long hedgers will hedge only for short periods of time and trade in and out of the market fairly rapidly. In some cases, long hedgers are willing to pay the price of a narrowing basis as a sort of insurance premium in order to gain the benefits of risk reduction. In an inverted market, long hedgers will consistently profit from hedging. For example, the crude oil futures market is usually inverted. If you purchase the deferred months and hold to maturity, in most cases your hedge will generate a profit.

When a hedger is long cash and short hedged, he is said to be "long the basis." The logic of the term "long the basis" corresponds to the logic of a bull spread. Both are profitable where the nearby contract (cash position) gains on the deferred futures contract. In a carrying charge market, when cash gains on futures, this is the same as basis narrowing. In an inverted market, when cash gains on futures, this is the same as basis widening. In either case, the short hedger will profit when cash gains on futures and lose money when cash loses ground to futures.

When a hedger is short cash and long hedged, he is said to be "short the basis." The logic of the term "short the basis" corresponds to the logic of a bear spread. Both are profitable when the nearby contract (cash position) loses ground to the deferred futures contract. Profits result from cash losing ground to futures. In a carrying charge market, cash losing to futures is the same as a widening basis. In an inverted market, it is the same as a narrowing basis. In either case, the long hedger will profit when cash loses to futures and lose money when cash gains on futures.

# SHORT HEDGE

Suppose that on September 1 a New York heating oil distributor purchases 168,000 gallons of heating oil for $.50 per gallon. He hedges by selling four December heating oil futures contracts at $.56 per gallon. The basis at the time the hedge is established is $.06 per gallon and, because carrying charges for heating oil are close to $.02 per month, the $.06 basis represents full carrying charges. (Convergence typically occurs near the beginning of the delivery month. Thus, in September, there are three months to convergence on the December contract.)

The heating oil distributor has the expectation that basis will narrow by about $.02 per month. Once the futures position has been established, the heating oil inventory position is hedged. Suppose that two months later, on November 1, the cash price of heating oil decreases by $.05 per gallon to $.45. However, the futures price fell by more than $.05 because the basis narrows by $.02 per month for a total price decrease of $.09. The futures price on November 1 is $.47 per gallon.

The distributor lost $.05 per gallon in inventory value but gained $.09 on the futures position. The distributor's position before and after the hedge is illustrated as follows:

| Date | Cash | Futures | Basis |
|------|------|---------|-------|
| 9/1 | Long 168,000 gallons of heating oil @ $.50/gallon | Sell 168,000 gallons (4 contracts) of Dec futures @ $.56/gallon | $.06 |
| 11/1 | Sell 168,000 gallons heating oil @ $.45/gallon | Buy 168,000 gallons (offset) of Dec futures @ $.47/gallon | $.02 |
| | Loss on cash = $.05 x 168,000 = –$8,400 | Gain on futures = $.09 x 168,000 = +$15,120 | |
| | | Net profit on hedge –$8,400 + $15,120 = +$6,720 | |

Notice that the basis narrowed by $.04 over a two month period and the short hedge generated a profit of $.04 per gallon. The effect of this is that the distributor got the futures market to pay his $.02 per month storage cost of heating oil. Also notice that the short hedger was long the basis and cash gained on futures by $.04 per gallon.

In the above example, it was assumed that the hedger was located in New York, which is the delivery point of the heating oil futures contract. Thus, it was safe to assume that location basis was zero and that basis was comprised solely of storage basis. This was done for illustrative purposes only. The existence of location basis would cause basis to be larger, but cash and futures prices would converge at the same rate and thus the profits or losses resulting from a hedge would not be affected.

Because short hedgers gain and long hedgers lose when basis narrows in a carrying charge market, there is much more of an incentive for hedging a long cash position than there is a short cash position. For this reason, there are usually more short hedgers who participate in futures markets than long hedgers. Long hedgers are usually in futures contracts for short time periods, and long hedging closely resembles risk-reduction hedging. Long hedgers are willing to bear the risk of unsystematic changes in basis but not of systematic changes for long hedging periods.

# SELECTIVE OR ANTICIPATORY HEDGING

In all of the hedging examples so far, it has been assumed that the hedger had no expectations as to the future direction of change of cash and futures prices. The hedger is typically willing to forgo the possibility of a favorable price change in order to reduce the potential loss of an adverse price move. Hedging allows a firm the freedom to pursue its line of business without having to worry about forecasting prices in the future.

Sometimes cash market participants have very definite opinions about the future level of cash prices. In some circumstances hedgers will hedge only when an adverse price move is expected. When favorable price moves are expected, the hedger will not hedge and thus will attempt to profit from the expected price move. Of course, if the forecast is incorrect the appropriate profit penalty will be imposed by the market. Sometimes hedgers will hedge only part of their cash positions, choosing to speculate on the unhedged portion.

Long hedgers with short cash positions will not hedge when prices are expected to fall and will hedge when prices are expected to rise. Short hedgers with long cash positions will hedge when prices are expected to fall and not hedge when prices are expected to rise.

Little is known about the effectiveness of selective hedging. On the one hand, because cash prices can be expected to follow a random walk, it is unlikely that many people can consistently forecast the direction of change in prices. The evidence on the profitability of speculators reinforces this notion. For indeed, selective hedging is merely speculation in the cash market; a failure to hedge a cash position is the same as speculating on cash prices. On the other hand, cash market participants are those most likely to be familiar enough with the working of the cash market to be able to forecast prices.

# STRIP HEDGING

Most hedging strategies involve the purchase or sale of a given quantity of futures in one particular month. However, some market participants need a more dynamic and flexible strategy to hedge several consecutive months forward. Thus, in 1995, NYMEX developed strip trading, also known as calendar strips, which gives energy companies the ability to lock in an average price for several months at a time by simultaneously opening a futures position in each of the months to be hedged through one transaction. A four month strip, for example, consists of an equal number of futures contracts for each of four consecutive months at a price differential to the previous day's settlement prices of those four contract months. The differential is determined by open outcry.

As an example, a trade involving 50 crude oil futures contracts for each of four calendar months beginning in January might be executed at $.10 a barrel above the previous day's settlement prices for January, February, March, and April, respectively. The buyer would receive 50 long crude oil futures contracts for the four consecutive months at $.10 above the previous day's settlement prices, while the seller would receive 50 short crude oil futures contracts for the four consecutive months at the same differential to the previous day's prices. The trade would clear at the following prices:

| Month | Quantity | Previous Day's Settlement Price | Today's Trade Price |
|---|---|---|---|
| January | 50 | $15.25 | $15.35 |
| February | 50 | $15.35 | $15.45 |
| March | 50 | $15.45 | $15.55 |
| April | 50 | $15.55 | $15.65 |
| Average | 200 | $15.40 | $15.50 |

## HEDGING IN ENERGY FUTURES

The existence of energy futures contracts offers hedging potential for many different businesses which operate in the energy arena. For instance, futures markets are useful in many different situations that involve protecting cash market sales against the effects of declining prices.

Futures markets may be used as an aid in fixed-price bidding because prices quoted may be made based on the prices of futures contracts near the delivery date of the product. For instance, suppose a marketer has recently purchased gasoline from his supplier. He cannot fix the price to his customer until he makes delivery. The marketer wishes to lock in a profit margin between his fixed purchase cost and his anticipated sales price. The solution to this problem is to agree to deliver gasoline to the customer at a price equal to the NYMEX settlement price on the day of delivery. The marketer will then sell an equivalent quantity of gasoline futures in the nearest trading month subsequent to the anticipated sale date. On the delivery day, when the marketer buys the physical barrels in the cash market, he will also buy back the gasoline futures at the then current price level. By this procedure, the marketer is able to quote a firm price to his customer and to lock in a profit margin between his fixed purchase cost and his anticipated sales price.

Suppose the marketer operates on a $.03 profit margin and that the December futures contract is selling at $.50 per gallon in September. The marketer will quote a price of $.53 per gallon to his customer. If prices (and thus his costs) increase, the long futures contracts will generate a profit which offsets the marketer's higher purchase price, and he is able to maintain the $.53 selling price to his customer.

Another use of futures is by refiners who wish to lock in the value of refined products. Refiners often have long-range contracts for the supply of crude oil. Typically, refiners are concerned that falling cash market prices will diminish the value of refined products like heating oil and gasoline. The solution to this problem is to sell heating oil and/or gasoline futures in quantities and trading months that approximate expected output and sale of refined products. As the refined products are produced and sold to customers, buy back the equivalent quantity of futures contracts.

Often refiners will operate much like a crack spread when the futures prices of refined products rise sufficiently above crude prices. Since they own crude oil, which is being refined, refiners can often lock in a very favorable profit margin when futures prices rise sufficiently above the equivalent cash market crude oil prices.

Electric generating companies can sell futures contracts to lock in a specific selling price for the power they intend or expect to produce in future months. Conversely, power purchasers, such as utilities or major corporations, can buy futures to protect their own purchase price. In addition, power marketers, who have exposure on both the generating and delivery sides of the market, can hedge with futures to reduce risk by buying or selling futures contracts.

The explosive growth of NYMEX's natural gas futures market has allowed marketers, producers, industry buyers, independent power producers, and gas and electric utilities to better manage price and supply risk. In fact, by using the resources of the futures market, gas marketers have been able to offer new purchasing strategies to their customers.

Sometimes the end-users of product want to choose the product prices they wish to pay. In these cases, suppliers may bid a job on the basis of a profit margin over and above the price of the futures contract, which is purchased at the time the end-user chooses. Suppose a municipality thinks that heating oil prices will decline in the future. The supplier will agree to deliver heating oil at the futures price plus its margin of, for example, $.03 per gallon, and will agree to purchase futures contracts for the customer at the time the customer decides to fix the price. If the end-user postpones locking in his price and if prices do indeed fall, the customer will receive the heating oil at a lower price. But if the price increases the customer will have to pay more. In either case the supplier receives his normal margin and is not subject to price risk.

Oil producers can use futures markets to hedge the price of crude oil in the ground. By selling crude oil futures contracts, producers protect against a fall in crude prices. In addition, producers will often borrow from banks against future crude production. The ability to lock in future selling prices provides a great deal of comfort to bankers. When banks loan money against future production they suffer a loss in the value of their collateral when crude prices decrease.

Futures contracts are also useful in facilitating swap transactions in different locations. Suppliers on the West Coast may obtain current supply in their location and concurrently use futures markets to lock in the price of product in the Northeast. Similarly, various grades of crude oil may be swapped for crude oil obtained on the NYMEX crude oil futures market which calls for delivery in Cushing, Oklahoma.

## SOME CAVEATS ON HEDGING

In order for energy futures contracts to be useful in hedging, their prices must be systematically related to local cash prices. Unfortunately, little has been published about the relationship between energy futures prices and cash energy prices at various locations around the country. Thus, a beginning point in any hedging program is to carefully research this relationship for the trader's location. Such a research program will involve a correlation analysis between futures prices and local cash prices. A history of daily futures prices is available from most futures commission merchants, especially those who specialize in energy futures. One would usually use the first nearby futures contract in conducting such an analysis. The researcher will have to generate a historical series of local cash prices.

The concepts of correlation and correlation analysis are quite familiar. Correlation is an indication of the relationship between two economic variables. A correlation coefficient is a number between −1 and +1 which measures the strength of the relationship. A negative or minus correlation coefficient is an indication of an inverse or negative relationship, and a positive correlation coefficient is an indication of a direct or positive relationship between the variables.

A related and very useful statistical tool is the coefficient of determination, also known as $R^2$. For a simple two-variable relationship, it is calculated by simply squaring the correlation coefficient. The $R^2$ coefficient is a number between zero and one that is also a measure of the strength of the relationship between the two economic variables involved. But it has a further interesting interpretation—it is the percentage of the variability of one of the economic variables which is "explained" by the other variable. In a futures market context, the $R^2$ term is interpreted as the amount of risk reduction that may be achieved by using futures contracts.

For instance, suppose a properly estimated correlation coefficient between cash and futures prices is .9. This means that, on average, 81% of the risk of cash market price changes can be offset by assuming a futures position opposite to the cash market position. If the correlation were .7 then only about 50% of the cash price risk could be eliminated with a properly constructed futures position.

An intuitive interpretation of a .8 coefficient of determination ($R^2$) would be as follows: suppose a particular cash position is subject to price risk of about ±10% around its average price. If a futures position is assumed that offsets (hedges) the cash position, then the resultant combination would be subject to a price risk of about ±2% assuming a .8 coefficient of determination.

Thus, a beginning point in examining the usefulness of energy futures for hedging local cash prices is to look at the correlation between cash prices in the local market and energy futures prices. However, caution should be exercised. The proper approach to this problem is to look at the relationship between cash and futures price changes and not the relationship between cash and futures price levels. When assuming a futures position, the gains and losses result from price changes. Price levels are irrelevant to the analysis.

Each potential trader/hedger should analyze the relationship between his cash prices and the appropriate futures contract for as long a time period as data are available. Local cash prices and the prices of the nearby and several deferred futures contracts should be plotted over time. The difference between the prices of the various futures contracts and the local cash price should also be examined. The basis should also be plotted and carefully analyzed. Such an analysis will give the analyst a feel for the important relationships and clues to possible profitable trades.

There are other caveats involved with hedging. Futures contracts are written for standardized amounts of product, for example, 42,000 gallons of gasoline. Usually the hedger will not want to hedge an exact multiple of the contract amount. This subjects the hedger to some small additional risk because he can seldom match cash and futures positions exactly.

Another element of price risk is quality uncertainty. Each futures contract is standardized and the quality of the goods deliverable against the contract is specified precisely. The futures market will price the contract on the basis of the price of the deliverable grade of the commodity. Should the actual cash position hedged not match the deliverable grade of the contract, then the price of the cash position may not move exactly opposite that of the futures contracts.

Hedgers are seldom able to time hedges perfectly. The futures part of a hedge may be lifted prior to liquidating the cash position because the liquidation process may take some time, whereas the futures position is eliminated almost instantaneously.

There is another dimension of the timing problem that is more important. The futures part of most hedges is eliminated by the offset procedure rather than by the delivery process. Few hedgers will carry a futures position into the delivery month of the contract but will offset the futures position prior to expiration. Before the expiration date of the futures contract, the cash and futures prices of a commodity may differ and these prices may change differently. When this occurs, basis changes and the hedger is subject to the risk of a change in basis.

## CROSS-HEDGING

Futures contracts are traded for a fairly limited set of commodities. Sometimes, futures contracts may be used to hedge the price risk of related commodities for which no futures contract is traded. This is called cross-hedging and a major consideration is whether the price of the futures contract used is highly correlated with the cash price of the commodity to be hedged.

Examples of cross-hedging would be the use of the heating oil contract to hedge aviation fuels as well as other grades of diesel fuel or residual fuel oil. Similarly, chemical companies often use the heating oil, natural gas, or propane futures markets to hedge chemical feedstocks.

There are two approaches to cross-hedging. The first is what is called a naive hedge and the second is based on a hedge ratio. In a naive hedge, one merely purchases or sells futures contracts with a total dollar value equal to the total dollar value of the cash market position to be hedged. For instance, suppose the current market price of jet fuel is $.60 per gallon and an airline wishes to hedge the future purchase of 210,000 gallons. The jet fuel has a total value of $126,000 ($.60 x 210,000 gallons). Suppose further that the current price of a 42,000 gallon heating oil futures contract is $.50 per gallon. The naive hedge procedure would be to purchase 6 heating oil futures contracts with an expiration date shortly after the desired purchase date of the jet fuel. The total dollar value of the futures position would be $126,000 ($.50 x 42,000 x 6). If it is assumed that the prices of jet fuel and heating oil are highly correlated, any increase or decrease in the cost of jet fuel will be offset by an approximately equal decrease or increase in the value of the futures contracts.

A more sophisticated hedging strategy is to estimate the historical price relationship between the commodity of interest and the price of the futures contract. This estimated relationship is then used to construct the proper "hedge ratio" which is a convenient way to express the size of the hedging position:

$$Hedge\ Ratio\ =\ \frac{dollar\ size\ of\ futures\ position}{dollar\ size\ of\ the\ cash\ position}$$

A naive hedge is simply the equivalent of a hedge ratio of $-1$. It is easy to show that the proper hedge ratio is the slope of the regression line with the price of the futures contract as the independent variable and the price of the hedged commodity as the dependent variable.

$$Hedge\ Ratio\ =\ \frac{-\ co\text{-}variance\ (F,\ S)}{Variance\ (F)}$$

where F and S represent changes in futures and spot prices.

The negative sign simply implies a short position in the futures contract against an implied long position in the spot market, or vice versa. Suppose a hedge ratio is estimated using ordinary least squares and is found to be $-1.5$. A $1 million position in the spot market would be hedged using a futures position with a total value of $1.5 million.

Hedging represents a sound, economically viable mechanism for reducing the risk of changes in energy prices. Both suppliers and purchasers of energy-related products may employ hedging in one or more of its forms. In addition to the products for which there are contracts traded, buyers and sellers of related products like kerosene, chemical feedstocks and residual fuel oil may benefit from risk-reduction techniques in futures markets by selectively cross-hedging.

The energy futures market, which began twenty years ago with NYMEX's No. 2 heating oil futures contract, is still quite new, and, as a result, there are gaps in our knowledge of the nature and magnitude of basis risk in cross-hedging. Buyers and sellers in energy-related industries should become thoroughly versed in the operating mechanics of energy futures markets before attempting to operate in them.

# Introduction to Options on Futures

There is a huge global market in energy options. The New York Mercantile Exchange began trading crude oil options in November, 1986, and the International Petroleum Exchange followed with gas oil options in July, 1987. Collectively, the two exchanges report a compound annual growth rate since 1987 of about 20%. A major cause of the growth of the market for energy options has been the extreme levels of energy price volatility since 1987 and especially during the Gulf War period of 1990. In late 1990, crude oil price volatility exceeded 100% on an annual basis.

Options contracts may be used to speculate on energy prices as well as to reduce or eliminate energy price risk. There are many different strategies involving options, futures, and combinations of different types of options and futures that allow for almost unlimited speculative and risk-reducing positions. Thus, options offer great flexibility and potential profitability to the energy speculator or hedger. The phenomenal growth in energy options is testimony to their usefulness in reducing uncertainty and profiting from price changes.

Like futures contracts, options are also exchange traded contracts for the purchase or sale of product in the future. Unlike futures contracts, which carry both the right and the obligation to buy or sell product in the future, option contracts are asymmetrical; they carry the right but not the obligation to buy or sell. Thus, the most important feature of options is that they allow the holder to participate and profit from price changes in a specified direction but to avoid the losses associated with an adverse price move.

Because the payoffs to options are asymmetrical, the purchaser of an option must pay for the right to participate in a price move in the desired direction. Options have often been likened to insurance where the "insured" pays an insurance premium to the insurance company in order to avoid losses. In the case of options, the insurance premium is paid to the seller of the option in the form of the market price of the option, which is called, appropriately, the "premium."

Unlike futures, where potential losses are unlimited with adverse price moves, the purchaser of an option contract has losses limited to the amount of the option premium. Thus, the risk exposure of an option is predetermined and limited to the option premium. This feature has contributed greatly to the popularity of energy options.

Exchange traded energy option contracts give the holder the right to buy or sell a specific futures contract at a predetermined price at any time prior to the expiration of the option contract. This bears repeating: the most popular option contracts are exchange traded and call for the delivery of a futures contract, not actual wet barrels, etc. These are sometimes called futures options or commodity options.

Exchange traded commodity options are the most popular in terms of trading volume. This is because the futures prices are published and are instantaneously transparent to all market participants. If delivery occurs, the futures contracts may in turn result in the delivery of actual product. Because futures prices track cash prices well, the net effect is that exchange traded energy options are effectively options on actual product even though actual contracts are written in terms of futures contracts.

The most popular exchange traded options are options on futures contracts for crude oil, heating oil, unleaded gasoline, and natural gas on the New York Mercantile Exchange and Brent crude and gas oil on the International Petroleum Exchange in London. There are also options traded on four electric futures contracts and crack spreads (heating oil/crude oil and unleaded gasoline/crude oil).

# OPTIONS TERMINOLOGY

There are two types of options contracts—calls and puts. A call option gives the holder the right but not the obligation to buy a futures contract, and a put option gives the holder the right but not the obligation to sell a futures contract.

The purchaser of a call option is said to be long the option and is bullish on the underlying futures contract. The purchaser expects the price of the underlying futures contract to increase. Because the prices of futures contracts are closely related to the cash prices of the underlying commodities (wet barrels, etc.), in effect the purchase of a call option is a bet that the underlying commodity price will increase.

The purchaser of a put option is also said to be long the option and is bearish on the underlying futures contract. The purchaser expects the price of the futures contract to decrease. Puts are essentially bets that the underlying commodity price will decrease.

There are two parties to every option contract—the buyer and the seller, or writer. The option buyer (discussed above) gets the right to buy (call option) or sell (put option) a futures contract and pays some consideration called the option premium, or just the premium. The premium is the market price of the option. The seller of an options contract assumes the obligation to sell (call option) or buy (put option) an underlying futures contract at the option of the buyer of the option. In return for assuming this obligation, the seller or writer receives the option premium.

Unlike buyers whose risk is known and limited, option sellers face unlimited potential losses. Of course, option sellers may have cash market positions that offset the price risk of the options. As a result of the potentially unlimited losses, option writers are subject to margin requirements. The level of margin imposed changes with the volatility of the underlying commodity.

The call writer (seller) is said to be short the call and is exposed to the risk of price increases. The call writer is typically bearish or neutral on the underlying commodity price.

The put writer (seller) is said to be short the put and is exposed to the risk of price decreases. Put writers are typically bullish or neutral on the underlying commodity.

Options buyers get the right to buy or sell a futures contract at a fixed price called the exercise or strike price. The terms exercise and strike price are used interchangeably. Each options contract has a unique exercise price that is fixed for the term of the option. For instance, a call buyer may get the right to buy a futures contract on crude oil for $15 a barrel for three months. Similarly, a put buyer might get the right to sell a futures contract on gasoline at $.50 a gallon for four months.

Options expiration dates are typically one to three days prior to the expiration of the underlying futures contracts and, similar to futures, there are options expiration dates every month. At any point in time there are options expiring as far as about 12 months in the future. The bulk of trading activity is typically confined to the nearby options; typically those expiring within about three months.

The market price of the option is called the premium. Table 6–1 is a simulated price quote for three-month options on crude oil. The current market price of a three-month crude oil futures contract is $15 per barrel and each underlying futures contract calls for the delivery of 1,000 barrels of crude oil. The table shows premiums on a per barrel basis. Thus, the premium on the three-month call with a strike price of $15 per barrel is $1.50 per barrel. Since the option is on a futures contract for 1,000 barrels, the actual dollar price of the option would be $1.50 times 1,000 barrels or $1,500, plus commissions.

The three-month put option with a strike price of $14 per barrel has a premium of $1.05 per barrel and the total dollar market price of the option would be $1.05 times 1,000 barrels or $1,050.

| Exercise Price | Call Premium | Put Premium |
|:---:|:---:|:---:|
| $14 | $2.05 | $1.05 |
| $15 | $1.50 | $1.50 |
| $16 | $1.10 | $2.10 |

**Table 6–1** Crude Oil Premiums for Three-Month Options (Futures at $15)

Options premiums (P) consist of two components—the time value premium (TVP) and the intrinsic value (IV).

$$Premium = Intrinsic\ Value + Time\ Value\ Premium$$
$$or$$
$$P = IV + TVP$$

The time value premium is the price the option buyer is willing to pay to speculate that the price of the futures contract will increase above (call) or below (put) the strike price of the option. The intrinsic value is the built-in profit on the option.

For call options the intrinsic value (built-in profit) is the futures price (F) minus the strike price (S) if the futures price is above the strike price. The option allows the holder to buy for S dollars a futures contract with a current market price of F dollars. Symbolically:

$$IVc = F - S \text{ if } F > S$$

For call options, if the futures price (F) is greater than the strike price (S), then the option is said to be "in-the-money." The intrinsic value cannot be negative. If the futures price is less than the strike price then there is no built-in profit and intrinsic value is equal to zero.

$$\text{If } F < S, IVc = 0$$

In Table 6–1 the three-month call with a strike price of $14 is in-the-money by $1 because it allows the owner of the call to buy for $14 something (the futures contract) that is currently worth $15.

Because the option premium and the intrinsic value are known at any point in time, the time value premium may be calculated as the difference between the premium and the intrinsic value.

$$TVPc = Pc - IVc$$

For the three-month call with a strike of $14, the time value premium is calculated as the difference between the premium of $2.05 and the intrinsic value of $1 per barrel (F–S = $15 – $14) or $1.05:

$$TVPc = \$2.05 - \$1.00 = \$1.05$$

If the futures price is less than the strike price, a call option is said to be "out-of-the-money" and the intrinsic value is zero. In Table 6–1, the call with a strike price of $16 is out-of-the-money. When options are out-of-the-money and have no intrinsic value, the market price of the option (the call premium) is also equal to the TVP of the option. For instance, in Table 6–1, the three-month call with the strike price of $16 has no intrinsic value and the premium of $1.10 is all time value premium.

If the futures price and strike price are equal (F = S) then the call option is said to be "at-the-money." In Table 6–1, the call with the strike price of $15 is at-the-money. Similar to out-of-the-money options, at-the-money options have no intrinsic value and the premium is all time value premium.

The definitions and relationships are similar although reversed for put options. The put premium may also be thought of as the sum of the IV and TVP but a put option (an option to sell) is in-the-money when the price of the underlying futures contract is less than the strike price. The intrinsic value of a put option is:

$$IVp = S - F \text{ if } F < S$$

In Table 6–1, the three-month put option with an exercise price $16 per barrel is an example of a put option that is in-the-money. It allows the holder to sell for $16 a futures contract that has a current market price of $15 and is thus in-the-money by $1 (S – F = $16 – $15 = $1).

Similar to calls, the premium and intrinsic value of puts are known and the time value premium may be calculated as the difference between the premium and the intrinsic value. For the in-the-money put discussed above, the time value premium is calculated as follows:

$$TVPp = Pp - IVp = \$2.10 - \$1.00 = \$1.10$$

Put options are out-of-the-money if the price of the underlying futures contract is greater than the strike price and at-the-money if the futures price is equal to the strike price.

$$\text{If } F > S, IVP = 0$$

In-the-money and at-the-money put options have no intrinsic value (built-in profit) and thus put option premiums are all time value premiums. In Table 6–1, the put with a strike price of $15 is at-the-money and the put with a $14 strike price is out-of-the-money.

## OPTION PAYOFFS

The market prices of options (the premiums) increase and decrease as the prices of the underlying futures contracts change. Because these contracts are exchange traded, there is a ready market to sell contracts previously purchased and to purchase contracts previously written (sold).

Options premiums will reflect time value premiums and any built-in profit resulting from the option being in the money. Similar to futures contracts, it is not necessary to exercise an option in order to realize profits. However, exercise is always an alternative for the buyer of a put or call option.

Because futures contracts involve both the right and the obligation to buy or sell, eventually one of two alternatives must occur: either the futures contract must be offset or it must be exercised. There are no other alternatives.

For options contracts, there is a third alternative—abandonment. It is possible that the options contract could expire worthless. This occurs for call options when the price of the underlying futures contract is less than the strike price at expiration and for put options when the price is greater than the strike price at expiration.

An example is in order. Suppose a crude oil call option with a strike price of $15 is purchased. The price of the underlying futures contract is currently also $15 so the option is at-the-money. The agents for the buyer and seller meet on the floor of the exchange and negotiate a price of $1.50 per barrel, or $1,500 per 1,000 barrel contract.

Now, at expiration of the option, one of three things must happen. In order to see this you need another piece of information—at expiration, the time value premium of any option is equal to zero. This is because there is no more optionality, or no more time for the bet to come through. Thus, no one would pay money (TVP) to make a bet that has no time to run. This means that, at expiration, the option will either sell for its intrinsic value (if any) or it will be worthless.

For the call buyer, one of three things must be true at expiration:

1. The call option expires worthless. This will happen at any futures contract price of less than $15 per barrel. The option will have no TVP and no IV because it is out-of-the-money. The call buyer will lose $1.50 per barrel or $1,500 on the whole option—the original cost. The rate of return will be minus 100%.

2. The option is sold for its intrinsic value. Suppose the price of the futures contract at expiration is $17.50 per barrel. The option will be in-the-money by $2.50 and thus can be sold for $2.50 per barrel or $2,500 total. This generates a net profit of $1 per barrel or $1,000 total (the option cost $1.50 and is sold for $2.50 = net profit of $1.00). This is a 67% return ($1 per barrel profit /$1.50 cost per barrel).

3. The option is exercised by the call buyer. Assume that the futures price is the same as in 2. above: $17.50 per barrel. In this case, the call buyer

would take delivery of a long futures contract with a current value of $17.50 per barrel and the seller of the contract would pay an additional $2,500 in cash to the buyer. This amount represents the difference between the current futures price and the strike price of the option. It is no accident that the profit is the same as in 2. above. The net profit would be $1 per barrel or $1,000 on the whole contract.

The profit/loss on the above call option is depicted graphically in Figure 6–1. It is called a profit/loss graph.

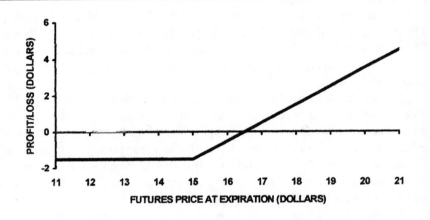

**Fig. 6–1** Call Buyer

The horizontal axis is the price of the underlying futures contract at the expiration of the option contract and the vertical axis is the per barrel profit or loss on the call option.

Notice that at any futures price below $15 per barrel at expiration, the call buyer loses the whole call premium of $1.50 per barrel. If the futures price is $16.50 at expiration, the call buyer will just break even because he will be able to sell the option for its intrinsic value of $1.50, which just covers the original cost of the option. At any futures price of more than $16.50 per barrel at expiration, the call buyer will make money.

For every option buyer, there is also an option seller. Similar to futures contracts, the payoffs on options are a zero sum game. When the buyer profits, the seller loses and vice versa.

Assume that the same three-month call on crude oil with a strike price of $15 is sold. The call seller pockets $1.50 per barrel or $1,500 total. Like call buyers, call sellers or writers must experience one of three outcomes at expiration:

1.  The call option expires worthless. This will happen at any futures price at expiration less than $15 per barrel. The option will have no TVP and no IV because it is out-of-the money. The call seller will profit by $1.50 per barrel or $1,500 on the whole 1,000 barrel option. This is the amount that was originally received when the option was sold.
2.  The option is purchased for its intrinsic value. Suppose the futures price at expiration is $17 per barrel. The option will be in-the-money by $2 and thus can be purchased for $2 per barrel, or $2,000 total. This generates a net loss of $.50 per barrel or $500 total because the option was originally sold for $1.50, or $1,500 total.

A clarification is in order—the call seller gets the option premium and assumes an obligation to sell a futures contract at the strike price. That obligation may be satisfied by purchasing an option identical to the one that was originally sold. The exchange's clearinghouse allows the seller to "offset" the short call with an identical long call. The seller would profit or lose by the difference in prices of the sold and purchased options.

3.  The option is exercised by the call buyer. In this case the call seller will deliver a long futures contract. The contract will have a current market price of $17 per barrel and the seller will also deliver $2,000 in cash to the buyer which represents the difference between the strike price ($15) and the current market price of the futures contract ($17). It is no accident that the net loss is the same as in 2. above.

The profit/loss for the call writer is depicted graphically in Figure 6–2.

At any futures price at expiration below $15 per barrel the call writer gets to keep the original premium of $1.50 per barrel because the option will expire worthless. If the futures price is $16.50 at expiration, the call writer will break even because it will cost $1.50 to purchase the option and satisfy the original obligation. This amount is equal to the premium received when the option was sold. Any futures price at expiration greater than $16.50 per barrel will result in a loss to the call writer. Since potential price increases are unlimited, potential losses to the call writer are also unlimited.

A word on delivery versus offsets. Similar to futures markets, the vast major-ity of option contracts are offset and actual delivery is a relatively rare occurrence. This is partially true because options contracts typically expire one to three days prior to expiration of the underlying futures contract and taking delivery of a futures contract is essentially the same as taking delivery of product. The net effect of this is that, similar to futures markets, option markets are essen-tially financial in nature and delivery of actual product or even futures con-tracts is relatively rare.

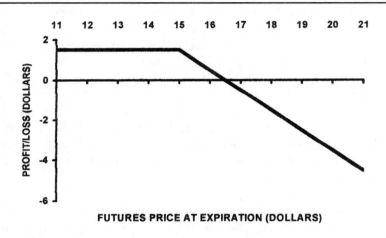

**FUTURES PRICE AT EXPIRATION (DOLLARS)**

**Fig. 6–2** Call Writer

Put options are similar to calls in that the time value premium is zero at expiration and the option will be worth the IV (if any) at expiration. Suppose a speculator buys the three-month put option on crude oil with a strike price of $15 per barrel. This option is at-the-money and, from Table 6–1, will have a mar-ket price (premium) of $1.50 per barrel.

Suppose the futures price is $15.50 at expiration. In this case the option will expire worthless because the futures price is above the strike price. (It wouldn't make any sense to exercise the option to sell for $15 when futures contracts can be sold in the open market for $15.50.) If the futures price is $13.50 at expira-tion the put buyer will just break even because the option can be sold for its intrinsic value ($1.50) which is exactly the price originally paid for the option. The put buyer makes money at any futures price at expiration below $13.50 at expiration, as depicted in Figure 6–3.

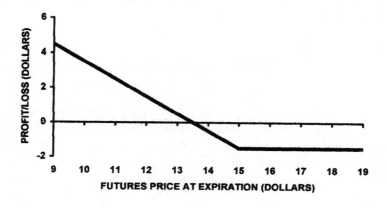

**Fig. 6–3** Put Buyer

The seller or writer of the same put option would get the $1.50 premium when the put was sold. The seller assumes the obligation to buy a futures contract (the put buyer gets the right to sell a futures contract at the strike price) at the strike price during the option period. The put seller's profit/loss position is depicted graphically in Figure 6–4.

At any futures price above $15 at expiration, the put seller gets to keep the whole $1.50 per barrel premium. The put seller will break even if the

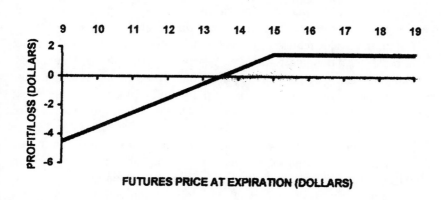

**Fig. 6–4** Put Writer

futures price is $13.50 at expiration and will lose money at any price below $13.50 at expiration.

# OPTION PRICING

Option traders use option pricing models, most notably the Black-Scholes model, to determine the "fair value" of options. The estimated option values are then compared to actual market prices to determine if arbitrage opportunities are potentially profitable. As a result of the activities of arbitrageurs, the market prices of exchange traded options seem to track well with values predicted by pricing models. It follows that there are no easy or riskless profits in the options markets just as there are no free lunches in futures markets.

Although the Black-Scholes model is beyond the scope of this book, it is possible to offer certain intuitive explanations for the model's important determinants. In the Black-Scholes model, the call option premium is determined by four factors:

1.  Market price relative to the strike price
2.  Time
3.  Volatility
4.  Interest rates

Recall that the option premium may be thought of as the sum of the time value premium and intrinsic value. From a theoretical point of view it is the time value premium that is of interest. The intrinsic value is a simple function of the interaction of the strike price and the price of the underlying futures contract.

The intrinsic value represents the minimum value of an option and is either zero or positive (an option cannot have a negative value). Consider Figure 6–5.

This graph is associated with the three-month crude oil option with a strike price of $15 per barrel. The dashed line is the intrinsic value line. Notice that it is zero below the strike price and increases dollar for dollar as the market price of the futures contract increases above the strike price.

The call premium is the solid curved line and represents the sum of the intrinsic value and time value premium. The time value premium may be thought of as the difference between the curved and dashed line. Notice that the time value premium is maximum when the option is at-the-money and decreases as the option moves further into the money as well as when it is further out-of-the-money.

There is an intuitive explanation for this relationship. Options that are well out-of-the-money have a relatively low probability of coming into the money and making a profit for their purchasers. Consequently, potential purchasers are not willing to pay very much to speculate that the price of the underlying futures contract will increase sufficiently to make the option profitable.

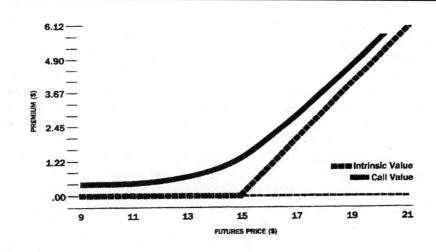

**Fig. 6–5** Call Value with Intrinsic Value Line

Options that are deep into the money have high premiums because of high intrinsic values but time value premiums tend to shrink as the option gets deeper into the money. The reason for this is associated with leverage. As options come into the money their intrinsic values and thus the total premiums increase. This means that speculators must invest more funds to purchase in the money options. As a result of this, the same dollar increase in the price of the underlying futures contract will produce smaller percentage gains because of the added money need to buy the option. Hence, options purchasers are willing to pay lower time value premiums for options in the money.

Both of these concepts may be illustrated mathematically with the aid of Table 6–1. It is customary to express option premiums as a % of the strike price to facilitate comparisons. The time value premium for the option that is at-the-money is $1.50, which is 10% of the strike price ($1.50/$15.00). The option with a strike price of $16 per barrel is out-of-the-money and the time value premium is 6.9 % of the strike price ($1.10/$16.00), while the in-the-money option has a premium of 7.5% of the strike price ($1.05/$14.00). The relationship is similar for put options. In Table 6–1 the at-the-money put has the greatest time value premium and the time value premiums decrease for options in- and out-of-the-money.

Options are wasting assets. Time value premiums decrease over time. This is the same as saying that time value premiums are an increasing function of time to expiration: the greater the time to expiration the greater the time value premium. Speculators are willing to pay more for options that have a longer time to expiration because there is a greater chance or probability that the market price will change sufficiently to generate a profit on the option.

As a useful "rule-of-thumb," other effects being equal, an option's time value premium varies with the square root of time. A six-month option can be expected to cost about 41% more than a three-month option (1.414 is the square root of two) and a one-year option twice as much as a three-month option (the square root of four being two).

All else being equal, there is a direct correlation between volatility and the market price of an option. Volatility is a measure of the amount by which an underlying futures contract is expected to fluctuate in a given period of time. Markets that move up or down very quickly are highly volatile. Markets that move up or down slowly are less volatile. Historical volatility is typically measured using a statistical measure called the standard deviation. Expected volatility is an important factor in option pricing.

As prices fluctuate more widely and frequently, the premiums for options on futures increase because increased volatility increases the chance or probability that the futures prices will substantially exceed the strike price for calls or be less than the strike price for puts. If market volatility declines, premiums for puts and calls decline correspondingly.

As an example, assume that the $1.50 time value premium on the at-the-money call option (strike price of $15) is based on a volatility estimate of 20%. If the volatility estimate jumped to 30%, an increase of half, the premium would also increase by half from $1.50 to $2.25.

Option pricing models utilize expected volatility as an input in estimating fair value. As a practical matter, since expected volatility is not observable, the models typically use historical volatility as a proxy and assume that the future will be like the past. Technically, historical volatility is the annual standard deviation of the log of the changes in the futures price, expressed in percentage terms.

Interest rates have a much smaller impact on option premiums than the other variables. An option effectively provides "free financing," since the holder of the option does not directly pay any carrying costs for the underlying phys-ical commodity or futures contract. On the other hand, the option buyer must pay the option premium up front. Generally, for options on futures these effects cancel each other out and the net impact of interest rates on energy option pre-miums is minimal.

The net effect of all of this is that options markets, on balance, do a good job of pricing options and at any point in time the default assumption is that options are fairly priced. This has serious implications, the most important of which is that option premiums appropriately reflect the risk of the underlying futures contract. Commercial hedgers looking to options markets to lay off price risk will find that the cost of doing so will sometimes seem very expensive. Moreover, because option premiums are a positive function of volatility, those periods when energy markets are the most volatile will also be the time when options are the most expensive. There are truly no free lunches in properly functioning futures and options markets.

# MARGIN REQUIREMENTS AND OPTION EXERCISE

The calculation of margin requirements on options is very complex. More-over, margin requirements imposed by exchanges may change on a daily basis. In general, what drives the margin requirements is volatility. As volatility increas-es so do margin requirements.

Exact margin requirements must be calculated using a computer program called SPAN. However, there are simple rules of thumb for figuring margin requirements for options. The option buyer simply pays the premium (the price of the contract). However, when writing (or selling) an option, margin is based on all related positions in the account. This can get confusing, but a general guide is that the margin required on a short option is approximately the premium collected, plus the underlying futures margin minus one half the amount the option is out-of-the-money, but not less than half of the futures margin. Each exchange has its own rules, which can be made more stringent by the Clearing Member or FCM.

Options are exercised at the option of the call or put buyer. Although exercise is a relatively rare occurrence for exchange traded options, the option to exercise and take delivery is always present. American options, which include all options discussed so far, may be exercised at any time up to the expiration date which is typically one to three days prior to the expiration of the underlying futures contract. European options may only be exercised at expiration.

There is another class of options not discussed so far—over-the-counter (OTC) or dealer options. These options are typically not standardized and involve delivery of actual product rather than a futures contract. The difference between the strike price and expiration price is settled at the average cash price during the expiration month. These are called Asian options.

# Energy Options Strategies

There is a wide variety of strategies involving calls, puts, futures and combinations of these instruments. Options may be used for speculative (trading) and/or risk reducing purposes. These will be discussed in turn although in practice the differences between trading options and futures and what is sometimes called hedging tends to blur.

To facilitate the discussion of some of the various trading strategies, a common set of options will be used. A simulated option quote for three-month heating oil options is presented in Table 7–1:

| Exercise Price | Call Premium | Put Premium |
|---|---|---|
| $.40 | $.063 | $.023 |
| $.43 | $.041 | $.040 |
| $.46 | $.022 | $.062 |

**Table 7–1** Heating Oil Premiums for Three-Month Options (Futures at $.43 per gallon)

111

# TRADING STRATEGIES

Options are very efficient vehicles for speculating on energy prices. In general, traders who expect price increases of the underlying commodity will choose call options. Such strategies are called bullish strategies because the terms "bull" and "bullish" are associated with optimism and price increases. Traders who expect price decreases will choose put options. These strategies are called bearish strategies because the terms "bear" and "bearish" are associated with pessimism and price decreases.

It is worth remembering that even though exchange traded options call for delivery of futures contracts, the principles of parallelism and convergence discussed in chapter 3 cause futures prices and cash prices to be highly correlated. The net effect is that option payoffs are also closely correlated with cash or spot market prices. Because of convergence of cash and futures prices at expiration, and because options expire essentially at the same time as the underlying futures contracts, the market prices of options will reflect the difference between cash prices and option strike prices at expiration.

# LONG PUTS AND CALLS

Figure 7–1 illustrates the profit/loss graphs for the purchase of two call options on heating oil. They are based on the at-the-money (strike price = $.43) and out-of-the-money (strike price = $.46) in Table 7–1. Figure 7–1 shows the profit/loss graphs for these two options and illustrates the differential costs and payoffs of at-the-money and out-of-the-money options: two of the choices available to traders.

The at-the-money option costs $.041 per gallon, or $1,722 per 42,000 gallon contract, and the out-of-the-money option costs $.022 per gallon, or $924 per contract. Notice that in Figure 7–1 the at-the-money option costs more but reaches break-even at a lower futures price at expiration.

For call options, the break-even point will be the strike price plus the premium paid for the option. For the at-the-money option, break-even will be $.471 per gallon. For the out-of-the-money option, break-even will be at $.482.

The out-of-the-money option costs less than the at-the-money option. Thus, it is cheaper to speculate on price increases and the potential loss is lower than the at-the-money options. However, there is also a lower probability that the option will generate a profit because its strike price is higher and the underlying futures price would have to change more in order to generate a profit.

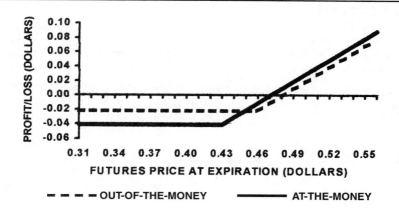

**Fig. 7–1** Long Calls

The premiums on put options are related to strike prices in the same general manner as call options. Options that are further out-of-the-money will have lower initial costs than options that are at-the-money and will also have a lower probability of generating a profit.

## SPREADS

A spread trading strategy involves taking a position in two or more options of the same type (*i.e.*, two or more calls or two or more puts). Option spreads are a means of speculating on the direction of commodity prices while at the same time limiting risk exposure.

Spread trading in options is somewhat different from spread trading in futures contracts and there is potential for confusion. Unlike options, spread trading in futures involves attempts to profit from changes in the relative prices of futures contracts, *i.e.*, a narrowing or widening of prices of futures contracts related in some fundamental manner. Option spreads involve attempts to profit from absolute changes in prices but with loss limitations.

# Bull spread

The bull spread is one of the better known and more frequently used option spreads. It is called a bull spread because the profit potential occurs when the underlying futures contract increases in price. It is created by buying a call option, usually at-the-money, and simultaneously selling a call option on the same futures contract with a higher strike price. Both options have the same expiration date.

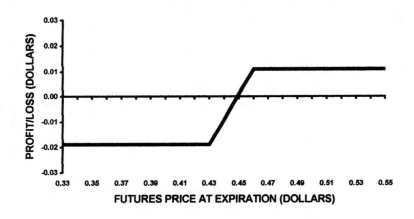

**Fig. 7–2** Bull Spread

The payoffs from a bull spread in heating oil calls are illustrated in Figure 7–2:

This spread was created by purchasing the at-the-money call options (strike price = $.43 per gallon) and simultaneously selling the out-of-the-money call (strike price = $.46).

A bull spread is a strategy that limits the trader's upside potential as well as downside risk. The premium received from selling the out-of-the-money call reduces the overall cost of speculating on price increases but also limits potential payoffs to the strike price of the out-of-the-money option. Before commissions, the long option cost $1,722 and the short option generated $924 in option income so that the net cost of the spread was $798 ($0.019 per gallon) and this is the maximum loss on the trade. The maximum profit potential occurs when the futures price is equal to the strike price of the out-of-the-money option at expiration. At that point the spread generates a net profit of $462 ($.03 per gallon times 42,000 gallons = $1,260, less the initial cost of $798). Above $.46 a gallon at expiration, the losses on the short call offset or negate profits on the long call.

There are other varieties of bull spreads. For instance, it is possible to create a bull spread where both calls are initially out-of-the-money. This is the most aggressive bull spread because it costs very little to set up and has a small probability of giving a relatively high payoff. Similarly, bull call spreads using in-the-money options are less risky but also generate relatively low payoffs.

The bull spread created using calls does not require a margin deposit. Bull spreads can also be created by buying a put option with a low strike price and selling a put option with a high strike price. Unlike call bull spreads, put bull spreads involve a positive cash flow to the trader up front and a payoff that is either negative or zero. This occurs because the premium received on the at-the-money put will be greater than the premium paid on the out-of-the-money put. Put bull spreads are subject to margin requirements set by the exchange where the spread is executed.

# Bear spread

A trader who enters into a bull spread is hoping that the underlying futures price will increase. By contrast, a trader who enters into a bear spread is hoping for a price decline. In Figure 7–3, put options on heating oil futures are used to construct a bear spread. The at-the-money put is purchased and the out-of-the-money put is sold.

Similar to bull spreads, bear spreads limit both the upside profit potential and the downside risk. The trader buys a put with a strike price of $.43 that costs $1,680 ($.04 times 42,000 gallons per contract) and gives up some of the profit potential by selling a put with a strike price of $.40. The short put generates $966 ($.023 per gallon) in income so that the net cost of the spread is $.017 or $714. The net cost is the maximum loss and the maximum potential gain occurs when the futures price is $.40 at expiration which generates a profit of $1,260 on the long option for a net profit of $546 because the short put will expire worthless. At any futures price at expiration below $.40 per gallon the losses on the short put will offset the gains on the long put.

Bear spreads can also be created using call options by purchasing a call at a high strike price and selling the lower strike price option. A bear spread from calls involves an initial cash inflow and is subject to exchange margin requirements.

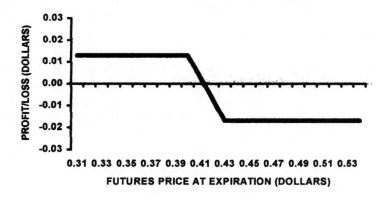

**Fig. 7–3** Bear Spread

# Butterfly spread

A butterfly spread involves options with three different strike prices. It can be created by buying two call options, one with a relatively low strike price (say the $.40 heating oil option) and one with a relatively high strike price (like the $.46 option) and simultaneously selling two call options with strike prices in between (like the $.43 heating oil option). The pattern for profits and losses is shown in Figure 7–4.

A butterfly spread generates a profit if the price of the underlying futures

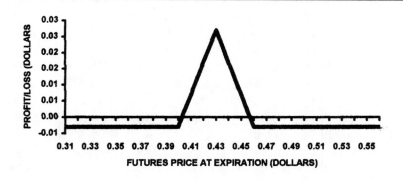

**Fig. 7–4** Butterfly Spread

contract does not change much and leads to a small loss if there is a significant move in either direction.

Other spread positions are possible. For instance, calendar spreads involve options with the same strike price and different expiration dates. Typically this involves selling a near dated option and buying an option with a longer expiration period. The profit and loss pattern is similar to that of a butterfly option. It is possible to create bull and bear calendar spreads as well as neutral calendar spreads.

## COMBINATIONS

A combination is an option trading strategy that involves taking a position in both calls and puts on the same underlying futures contract. A straddle involves a put and a call at the same strike price and the same expiration date. A long straddle requires the trader to buy a call and a put at the same strike price and expiration date. For instance, Figure 7–5 shows the profit/loss position resulting from the purchase of one three-month heating oil call and one three-month heating oil put, both with a strike price of $.43 per gallon.

The call costs $.041 per gallon ($1,722 total) and the put costs $.040 per gallon ($1,680 total). Thus the total cost of the combination is $.081 ($3,402 total).

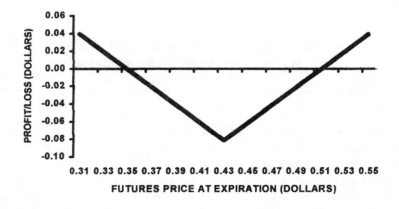

**Fig. 7–5** Long Straddle

In order for the long straddle to generate a profit, the underlying futures contract must change in price by at least $.081 per gallon.

Straddles are volatility plays. A long straddle is appropriate when the trader is expecting a large price move but does not know the direction of the move. Thus, long straddles are profitable in periods of unexpectedly high volatility. Of course, if the volatility is expected because the recent past has been volatile, then option premiums will be prohibitively expensive because premiums are positively related to expected volatility.

A short straddle involves the sale of a put and a call with the same strike price and the same expiration dates. A short straddle using the same three-month heating oil contracts with a $.43 strike price would generate $3,402 of option income and would generate a profit as long as the futures price changes by less than $.081 per gallon in either direction. The profit/loss graph for this short straddle position is depicted in Figure 7–6.

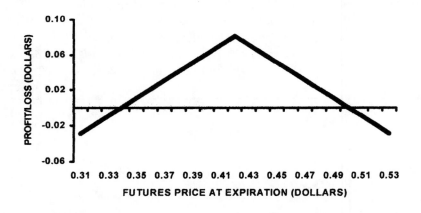

**Fig. 7–6** Short Straddle

Short straddles generate significant income and are subject to margin requirements. They are very risky because losses arising from a large move in either direction are unlimited.

A strangle involves the purchase of a put and a call with the same expiration dates and different strike prices. For instance, Figure 7–7 shows the profit/loss graph for a long strangle utilizing three-month heating oil options.

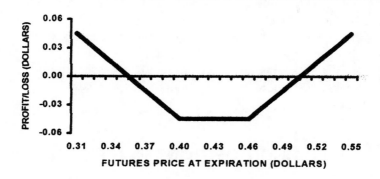

**Fig. 7–7** Long Strangle

Out-of-the-money puts and calls are purchased. The put with a strike price of $.40 per gallon costs $.023 and the call with a strike price of $.46 costs $.022 per gallon. The total cost of the trade is $.045 per gallon and $1,890 total for the two contracts.

As a strategy, a strangle is similar to a straddle. The trader is anticipating that there will be a large price movement but is uncertain as to the direction.

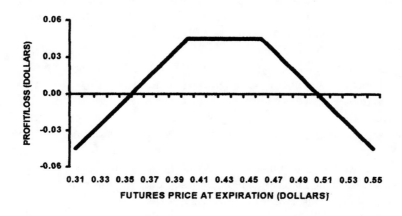

**Fig. 7–8** Short Strangle

With strangles, the futures price has to move farther to generate a profit but the cost is less than a straddle because out-of-the-money options are purchased. Because the options are out-of-the-money, they involve lower premiums.

The short strangle is illustrated in Figure 7–8. It may be sold by traders who believe that large price moves are unlikely. Like the short straddle, it generates income, involves a margin deposit and is risky because it may generate unlimited losses.

## HEDGING POSITIONS IN OPTIONS

It is possible to reduce the risk of cash or futures market positions by using put and call options. Although sometimes called hedge positions, in many cases, such trading is closer to insurance than hedging.

Here is how to think about the issues. One definition of hedging is "to protect by taking offsetting risks." In a futures market context, a true hedge involves assuming a futures contract opposite to the cash market position. When this is done, all price fluctuations are offset, even those that are favorable to the hedger. In essence, the hedger is saying that he is willing to forego favorable price moves in order to eliminate the possibility of unfavorable price moves. True hedgers typically are in some business related to cash markets and view futures markets as a risk reducing mechanism. Hedging may generate some profit as a result of a widening or narrowing of the basis, but the main motivation is to reduce risk.

There may be times when cash market positions are selectively hedged, i.e, the futures position is assumed only when the hedger has an opinion about the future course of cash prices. Although called a selective or anticipatory hedge, such positions involve a significant speculative element.

Options by their nature, are asymmetrical; they generate profits related to underlying futures or cash prices in only one direction. Because the profits generated are asymmetrical, there is a significant cost to buying either a put or call option. The cost, called the premium, is sometimes likened to an insurance premium.

Now here is the problem with options as a hedging position. True insurance, for instance home insurance, is in effect all of the time. You don't insure your house only when you are afraid of a fire, you insure it all the time. The problem is that if options are used on a consistent basis, like insurance, they are prohibitively expensive.

Options markets are very efficient at pricing the risk of underlying futures contracts and their associated cash market prices. In some sense, options premiums are "correct" in most situations and thus it is no accident that the true cost of insurance against price risk is expensive.

The commercial business or energy trader subject to price risk is left with two alternatives. Cash market risk may be selectively hedged by only assuming option positions when there is fear of adverse price moves. This involves a significant speculative element. The second alternative is to look for mechanisms to reduce the cost of hedging and/or to partially hedge.

It is good to keep these distinctions in mind during the following discussion. Several different hedge positions will be discussed involving options on crude oil futures contracts. Table 7–2 depicts simulated option premiums on crude oil options with a two-month expiration period. The premiums are simulated based on a relatively low expected volatility of underlying crude oil prices. It is assumed that the underlying futures contract is trading at $15 per barrel.

| Exercise Price | Call Premium | Put Premium |
|---|---|---|
| $14 | $1.25 | $.25 |
| $15 | $.50 | $.49 |
| $16 | $.25 | $1.24 |

**Table 7–2** Crude Oil Premiums for Two-Month Options (Futures at $15 per barrel)

# CAPS, FLOORS, AND COLLARS

A cap is the purchase of a call option to limit the cost of acquiring product in the future. For instance, oil refiners are subject to the risk of crude oil price increases. Essentially, refiners have a short cash market position. If crude prices increase, their costs increase and profits decrease, and vice versa. The profit/loss graph for a short cash position in crude oil is depicted in Figure 7–9.

Suppose that a refiner has decided to protect itself against an increase in crude oil prices. In practice, a series of call options with expiration dates as far as a year in the future will be purchased. For simplicity, the discussion will be limited to only two-month options.

The refiner needs to hedge about 100,000 barrels per month. The refiner could cap the cost of crude oil by buying call options with a strike price of $16 per barrel and a premium of $.25 per barrel, effectively limiting the cost of crude

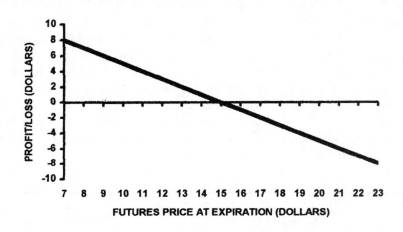

**Fig. 7–9** Short Cash Crude

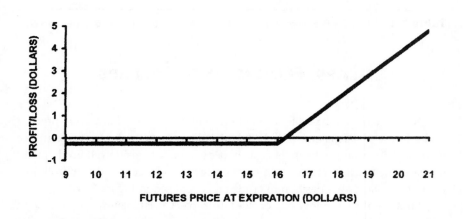

**Fig. 7–10** Crude Oil Cap at $16 per Barrel

oil to the strike price plus the option premium. The profit/loss graph for the two-month call/cap is shown in Figure 7–10.

Since the refiner is trying to protect 100,000 barrels per month he will buy 100 calls at the $16 per barrel strike price. The cost per contract will be $250 and the total cost of 100 contracts will be $25,000. This may be viewed as an insurance premium to cap his crude oil cost at $16.25 per barrel. The refiner will retain the benefits of a decrease in oil prices less the cost of the cap. To illustrate, the refiner's position in two months for a crude oil price increase and a crude oil price decrease is shown below:

|  | **Price Increase** | **Price Decrease** |
| --- | --- | --- |
| Spot Price | $18.00 / Barrel | $13.50 / Barrel |
| Futures Price | $18.00 / Barrel | $13.50 / Barrel |
| Cash Market Cost of 100,000 Barrels of Crude Oil | $1,800,000 | $1,350,000 |
| Less: Gain (Loss) on Options |  |  |
| Sales Price of Options | $200,000 | $0 |
| Purchase Price of Options | (25,000) | (25,000) |
| Net Gain (Loss) on Options | $175,000 | ($25,000) |
| Effective Total Cost of Crude Oil | $1,625,000 | $1,375,000 |
| Effective Per Barrel Cost of Crude Oil | $16.25 | $13.75 |

The sales price of the options associated with a price increase ($200,000) represents an intrinsic value of $2 per option because the cash price is $18 and the strike price is $16 per barrel. The purchase of the call put a cap on crude oil costs of $16.25 per barrel. Above this price, profits on the long call offset increased crude prices dollar for dollar.

A floor establishes a minimum price at which product may be bought or sold. It is simply a cap in reverse. The purchase of a floor involves buying a put to protect against a fall in product prices. If prices do fall, the profits generated by the long put will offset or negate some of the lost profits resulting from lower product selling prices.

For instance, in the fall a small heating oil refiner is concerned that warm weather will drive heating oil prices down. With three-month futures trading at $.43 per gallon, the refiner considers selling futures to lock in that price. However, if the weather is cold, prices could rise above $.43 and he would like to be able to earn the higher revenue.

The refiner decides to buy put options to protect against a fall in heating oil prices. Assume that from Table 7–1, the refiner is able to buy a put option with a strike price of $.43 per gallon for a premium of $.04 per gallon. The refiner needs to protect 840,000 gallons of heating oil to be produced in three months. As with the previous example, this one is over-simplified and in practice a series of puts could be purchased to protect prices as far as a year in the future.

The refiner buys 20 three-month puts with a strike price of $.43 per gallon for $.04 per gallon. The total cost of the position is $33,600 (20 contracts times 42,000 gallons per contract times $.04 per gallon). In three months, the refiner sells his supply commitments and liquidates his options position. If prices fall, the refiner has purchased a floor of $.39 per gallon (the put strike less the premium). If heating oil prices should increase, the refiner will be able to profit from the increase, less the cost of the puts. The following table illustrates these points for a price decrease and a price increase.

|  | Price Decrease | Price Increase |
|---|---|---|
| Three-Month Spot Price | $.36 / Gallon | $.55 / Gallon |
| Three-Month Futures Price | $.36 / Gallon | $.55 / Gallon |
| Cash Market Sales Revenue for | | |
|     840,000 Gallons of Heating Oil | $302,400 | $462,000 |
| Add: Gain (Loss) on Options | | |
|     Sales Price of Options | $58,800 | $0 |
|     Purchase Price of Options | (33,600) | (33,600) |
|     Net Gain (Loss) on Options | $25,200 | ($33,600) |
| Effective Total Revenue | $327,600 | $428,400 |
| Effective Per Gallon Revenue for Heating Oil | $.39 | $.51 |

The purchase of the put options places a floor under the revenue the refiner is to receive in the future while allowing him to participate in price increases. The cost of this "insurance" is $.04 per gallon. Of course, cheaper insurance could have been purchased by buying the three-month put option with the $.40 strike price. It would cost only $.023 per gallon and would provide a floor price of $.377 per gallon.

Caps and floors may provide upside price protection (caps) or downside price protection (floors) but at a cost that may seem prohibitive. A collar is a technique used to reduce these costs.

Return to the first example where the refiner used two-month crude oil options to protect against an increase in crude prices. The cost of this protection could be reduced or eliminated by selling a floor. By selling a put (floor), a commercial player fixes the minimum price that it will pay for energy, and thus gives up any chance of profiting from a fall in prices below a certain level. But the sum raised from the sale may be used to subsidize the price paid for upside insurance in purchasing calls.

For instance, selling a floor on two-month crude oil might involve selling a put option with a strike price of $14 per barrel and a premium of $.25 per barrel. The profit/loss graph associated with this strategy is presented in Figure 7–11.

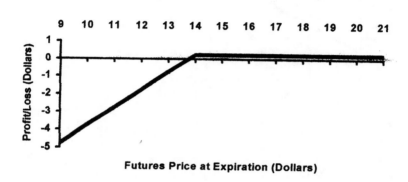

**Futures Price at Expiration (Dollars)**

**Fig. 7–11** Short Crude Oil Floor at $14 per Barrel

Above the strike price, the floor seller gets to keep the premium and the position generates losses if the futures price at expiration is below the strike price. However, because the refiner is short crude, decreases in crude prices generate gains on his cash position.

The combination of a call purchase (cap) and the sale of a put (floor) is called a collar. Collars, also sometimes called fences, limit the range of energy costs in the future to variations between the strike prices of the cap and the floor.

For instance, the refiner in the above example decides that it cannot afford to pay the cost of the cap (the $.25 per barrel premium). The refiner therefore decides to purchase the cap at $16 per barrel and to finance it through the sale of a $14 floor. This provides the refiner with a collar at zero cost as shown in Figure 7–12.

If the price of crude rises above $16, the refinery sells its cap and its effective cost of crude oil is $16. If the price of crude falls below $14, the refiner must buy back the floor and the effective minimum cost of crude is $14 per barrel. If crude prices stay between $14 and $16 per barrel, the refinery obtains its supplies at the market price.

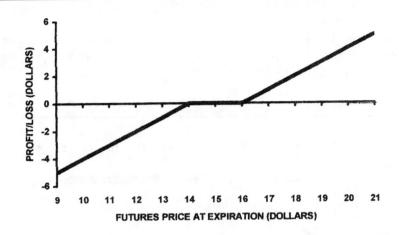

**Fig. 7–12** Zero Cost Collar

On the surface, using a zero cost collar may appear to be a very safe course of action for the refinery. It involves no up-front cost and offers no "speculative" return. However, if oil prices fall substantially, the refinery may end up paying much more for its feedstock than its competitors (who may lower prices aggressively as a result). The "zero cost" collar is really a "zero up-front cost" collar. True price insurance can only be obtained by purchasing a cap outright.

In the floor example, the heating oil refiner worried that product price decreases could implement a collar by pairing a short call position with the long put position. The short call generates revenues to pay for the put protection but limits profits resulting from price increases to the strike price of the call options.

# BULL AND BEAR SPREADS

Caps and floors are means of protecting against price increases and decreases but are expensive to implement. Zero cost collars are one means of coping with the expense. Bull and bear spreads are another.

A bull spread is a call that is partly financed by simultaneously selling another call with a higher strike price. A bear spread is a put that is acquired more cheaply by also selling a lower strike put.

For instance, a refiner who is short 100,000 barrels of crude oil in two months could buy 100 call options with a strike price of $15 per barrel. From Table 7–2, this would cost $.50 per barrel or $50,000 total, rather expensive protection. However, the refiner could simultaneously sell 100 call options with a strike price of $16 per barrel. The revenue would be $.25 per barrel so that the net cost of the spread would be $.25 per barrel or $25,000 total. The profit/loss graph for this strategy is presented in Figure 7–13.

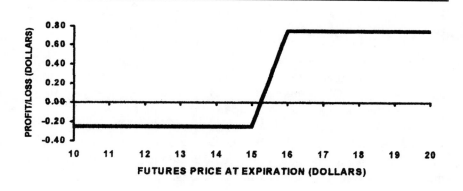

**Fig. 7–13** Bull Spread—Crude Oil

The refiner would reduce the cost of price protection by 50% (from $50,000 to $25,000) but give up protection above $16 per barrel. A price move above $16 per barrel would be viewed as less likely than a price move from $15 to $16 per barrel.

Like bull spreads, bear spreads can be used to reduce the cost of floors by selling a put option at a strike price below the floor price. Bull and bear spreads usually attract companies that would like to buy straight options, but which also want to pay a smaller up-front premium. To gain a saving they are willing to give up protection from some of the less likely or distant price movements.

## CRACK SPREAD OPTIONS

Crack spreads using futures contracts were discussed in chapter 5. The term crack spread is associated with the differences between input and output prices for refineries. Specifically, refineries use crude oil as inputs into the refining process and "crack" petroleum molecules into various refined products, principally gasoline and heating oil. Refinery margins are impacted when the prices of crude and refined products diverge because of differing supply and demand conditions in different energy markets.

Crack spreads using futures often reflect real world refining ratios. A popular spread is the 3-2-1 spread which uses the prices of three barrels of crude, two barrels of gasoline, and a barrel of heating oil to determine the spread. Another common spread uses the 5-3-2 ratio, and many other ratios are used as well. Hedging crack spreads with futures locks a market participant into a specific spread and thus requires the holder to forego favorable spread changes in order to eliminate the risk of an unfavorable spread change.

Crack spread options are also designed to protect the refining margin, while at the same time allowing refiners and other market participants to take advantage of favorable changes in the spread. Similar to other options, the cost of that asymmetrical position is the up-front option premium.

Essentially, a crack spread option is a combination of two options—one on crude oil and one on either heating oil or gasoline. Crack spread options trade with a one-to-one ratio of crude oil to heating oil or gasoline. They differ from conventional options in that a single option position results in two futures positions when the option is exercised. Suppose that crude oil is trading at $15 per barrel and that gasoline is trading at the equivalent of $19 a barrel ($.4523 per gallon times 42 gallons = $19 per barrel). The spread is $4 per barrel.

The unhedged producer loses if the spread decreases—that is, if the price of crude oil increases relative to the price of gasoline or the price of gasoline decreases relative to the price of crude oil. The producer could eliminate the risk of a narrowing of crack spreads by buying a put on the crack spread. Using the example above, the strike price of the long crack put would be $4. For a three-month option, the premium might be in the neighborhood of $.50 per gallon.

Like all puts, the option generates a profit if the price of the underlying instrument, in this case the spread, decreases in value. So if the crack spread narrows, say to $2.75, the long crack put will generate a net profit of $.75 per barrel after the $.50 premium. If the spread widens, the producer's option will expire worthless but he will profit from the widening because his cash margins will increase. Of course, as in other option positions used to reduce risk, the favorable move will be reduced by the cost of the option, in this case, $.50 per gallon.

# DERIVATIVES

Derivatives are contracts that derive their value from other instruments such as cash commodities, stocks or futures contracts. Technically, the exchange traded futures and options discussed so far are derivatives although common usage reserves the term "derivative" for other instruments only alluded to so far in this book.

The market for trading derivative contracts is comprised of dealers who are dispersed geographically and connected via computers and telephones. Unlike exchange traded derivative contracts, there is no central trading place. Essentially this is the market for dealer created contracts.

The most familiar dealer derivative contracts are forward contracts discussed briefly in chapter 1. Such contracts are not standardized and typically involve delivery of the underlying commodity. Dealers create unique forward contracts for each transaction and generally lay off some or all of their risk in the futures markets.

Dealers also make markets in options and swaps. Dealer options generally are not standardized and are generally cash settled. Their value at settlement is normally based on an average price over a period. The most common period is a calendar month. The average is calculated based on an index price derived from daily futures settlement prices or from energy industry pricing publications.

Swaps are dealer arranged contracts that are sometimes called "contracts for differences" or "fixed for floating" contracts. These terms summarize well the essence of these arrangements.

As an example, one party, say a producer, could sell a swap to lock in a sales price. The producer and an intermediary could agree to exchange the difference between a fixed price, say $15 a barrel, and a reference floating price derived from an oil pricing publication or from one of the futures markets.

For the period agreed upon, the producer receives from the intermediary the difference between the fixed price and the floating price if the latter is lower. If the floating price is higher, the difference is paid by the producer to the intermediary. A simple formula for calculating the difference is:

*Contracted Monthly Volume x (Fixed Price minus Floating Price)*

For example, a crude swap for a particular month might be:

*100,000 bbl x ($15 – $14.20) = $80,000*

In this case, the seller of crude took a $15 swap for 100,000 barrels a month and would receive $80,000 this particular month. If the floating price had been higher, the producer would have paid the difference to the intermediary.

This illustrated only the simplest or "plain vanilla" swap. There are swap contracts developed for a wide array of different situations and even options on swaps, called swaptions. The potential combinations are nearly endless.

# Technical Factors

The purpose of technical analysis or "charting" is to predict the prices of commodity futures contracts. Charting techniques are mainly short-term techniques. Technicians use charts of historical commodity futures contract prices and the corresponding volume and open interest numbers to identify price trends and repetitive "patterns" to predict future price levels. Technicians operate on the assumption that if recent price changes have formed a pattern similar to patterns formed in the past, then the prices of contracts in the future will probably duplicate the price changes that followed these patterns in the past. In other words, the prices of commodity futures contracts follow consistent and repetitive patterns and these patterns are a reliable basis for price forecasting. The assumption is that what happened yesterday is useful in predicting what will happen today. A second assumption is that trends exist which last for time periods long enough to be identified and therefore long enough to generate profits.

The usefulness of charting techniques to predict future price levels is contradicted by large amounts of academic research on commodity and security prices. In general, this research falls under the heading of what is called the random walk hypothesis (RWH). The RWH suggests that successive price changes are (1) independent (random) and (2) identically distributed. In a practical sense this means that prices have no memory. Because new information relevant to price formation arrives randomly and is rapidly reflected in prices, price changes are random because information arrival is random.

The vast preponderance of the evidence in this "argument" between technicians and academics favors the academic position. The evidence strongly suggests that price changes are statistically random and that technicians are not able to predict prices. Of course, since at any point in time prices are as likely to go up as they are to go down, by definition technicians will be right 50% of the time. When they are right, by chance, technicians believe that they predicted the change.

There are instances when technicians appear to make money. In those cases it appears as though the technical analyst is using some other skill than just chart interpretation in making a profit. At any rate, it is certain that the ability to make money speculating in futures markets is exceedingly difficult and casual technical analysis is not useful in earning excess profits.

Does this mean that the potential energy futures trader should ignore technical analysis completely? The answer to this question is no. Technical analysis may still be useful but in different ways than those suggested by technicians.

In spite of its lack of academic acceptance, many traders attempt to use charts. During those periods when there is a dearth of fundamental information, technical traders may temporarily have an inordinate impact on market prices. In such instances, technical analysis becomes a self-fulfilling prophecy. If many traders believe that prices will increase because of a technical pattern and those traders purchase futures contracts, then the very act of attempting to take advantage of the perceived trend may cause it to occur. Thus, the potential trader may gain useful insights into the market by understanding the motivations of other market participants.

In addition, charts are useful tools in generating information. Charts allow the trader to organize and uncover useful insights about market behavior and increase the trader's understanding of futures markets. Thus, one doesn't have to believe in technical analysis in order to use charts to gain insight and an overview of what has happened and what is currently happening. Such information can be useful in choosing which contract month to use for hedging, in understanding the cause of basis changes, and in other instances when a pictorial view is helpful.

# VOLUME AND OPEN INTEREST METHODS

A favorite technical tool is to examine the relationship between price, open interest, and volume. It is generally recognized that prices change when supply and demand change. Changes in volume and open interest are associated with changes in the supply and demand for futures contracts. Thus, technicians often analyze volume and open interest in attempts to predict price changes.

Volume refers to the aggregate number of contracts traded in a given period. Open interest is the total purchase or sale commitments outstanding. At any point in time the number of contracts outstanding which are long is equal to the number of contracts outstanding which are short. This is true because for every buyer in futures markets there is also a seller.

General rules have been formulated to indicate how changes in volume and open interest are related to price changes. In general, when a major price advance is under way, volume tends to increase on rallies and decrease on price declines. During a price decline, volume tends to increase on price declines and decrease on rallies. In addition, volume tends to expand sharply as the market nears the bottom or the top.

If open interest expands when prices are increasing, it is an indication that new buyers have entered the market. If open interest declines when prices are advancing it is an indication that the advance has been fueled by short covering and that the advance is technically weak. If open interest declines when prices decline it is likely that the decline has been fueled by discouraged buyers who are liquidating their unprofitable positions, which leaves the market relatively strong technically.

These relationships may be summarized as follows—if prices are up and (1) volume and open interest are up, the market is strong; (2) volume and open interest are down, the market is weak. If prices are down and (1) volume and open interest are up, the market is weak; (2) volume and open interest are down, the market is strong.

A strong or a weak market is an indication of whether or not the indicated trend is likely to continue and thus supposedly provides buy and sell signals to traders.

## CHARTING

The most common form of chart is the bar chart. To construct a bar chart, the technical analyst graphs each period's price activity (price range and settlement price) as a vertical line with a crossbar indicating the settlement price. The horizontal axis of a bar chart represents time. Monthly, weekly, and daily bar charts are used at different times depending on the market perspective desired. In futures markets, the most frequently used charts are daily bar charts. An example is presented in Figure 8–1.

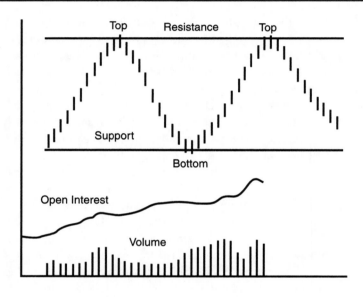

**Fig. 8–1** An Example of a Daily Bar Chart

In bar charts, weekend days are omitted. In addition, bar charts typically contain daily volume and open interest information. Volume data are represented in the form of vertical bars at the bottom of the chart. Open interest is plotted as a horizontal line, also at the bottom. Typically, each contract month of each futures contract of interest to the analyst is charted. Many technicians subscribe to charting services that use sophisticated equipment to construct charts.

Technical analysts attempt to recognize and interpret sequences of price patterns in attempts to predict futures price movements. Even though the description of the patterns lacks precision and interpretation is very subjective, technicians have developed some uniform terms to describe repetitive patterns. We present some of these below.

## Channels and trend lines

The trend is loosely defined as the direction of a commodity price. The daily price ranges of commodity futures tend to be bounded by straight lines, so that lines drawn to connect successive highs or lows often reveal trends of differing lengths. Thus, the trend is measured by "a trend line" connecting trading tops and bottoms. Sometimes the lines connecting the highs and lows are roughly parallel, creating a "trend channel," which indicates that the market is in a major up trend or down trend. Trend lines and a channel trend are illustrated in Figure 8–2 and Figure 8–3.

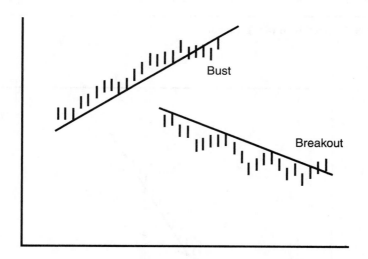

**Fig. 8–2** Trend Lines

## Momentum

Momentum is measured by the slope of the trend line with steeper lines denoting more momentum and flatter slopes less momentum as shown in

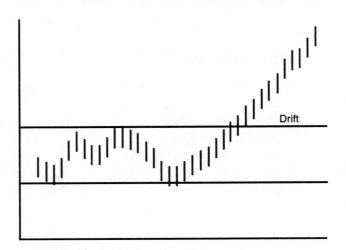

**Fig. 8–3** Channel Trend with Breakout

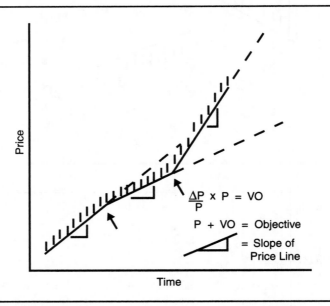

**Fig. 8–4** Slope/Price Velocity

Figure 8–4. In general, it is believed that the greater the momentum (slope) of a trend the more likely it is to reverse itself.

## Reversal

A trend is said to be in reversal when the succession of peaks and troughs no longer continues in the same direction as the recent past.

## Support and resistance areas

The market sometimes rallies and then falls back to a previous price area. This may occur several times. These downside price areas are called support areas. Similarly, if the market rallies in the same general area and then falls back, the chartist terms the upside areas a resistance area. Support and resistance areas are labeled in Figure 8–1.

## Head-and-shoulders pattern

The head-and-shoulders pattern is supposedly an indication of a major reversal in the market direction. The formation consists of four phases—development

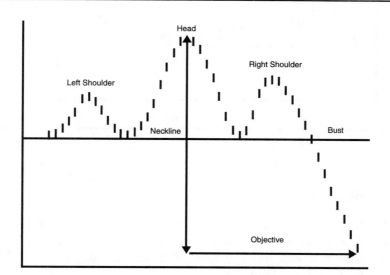

**Fig. 8–5** Head and Shoulders

of the left shoulder, development of the head, the right shoulder, and penetration of the neckline. The head and shoulders is complete only when the neckline is penetrated. The head and shoulders occurs in a rising market and the inverted head and shoulders occurs in a declining market. The head-and-shoulders pattern is illustrated in Figure 8–5.

## Gaps

Gaps represent a price area in which the market did not trade. There are several types of gaps including the common gap, the breakaway gap, the runaway gap, and the exhaustion gap. Several gap patterns are illustrated in Figure 8–6.

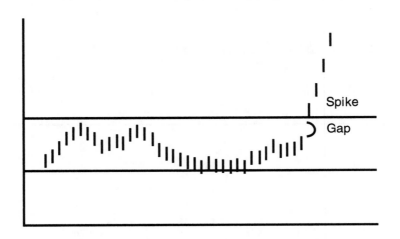

**Fig. 8–6** Gap Breakout

## Triangles

Triangles in many forms appear in commodity charts. The most common triangle patterns are the consolidation triangle, the ascending triangle, the descending triangle, and the triangle with a descending top. Triangles are illustrated in Figure 8–7 and Figure 8–9.

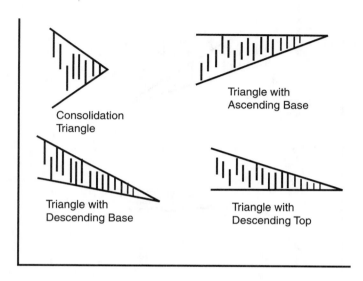

**Fig. 8–7** Triangles

## Pennants

Pennants consist of a major trend line or a "pole" and a descending triangle pattern. Such patterns supposedly represent price consolidations and give an indication of "equilibrium levels." This pattern is illustrated in Figure 8–8.

Technicians often look for and interpret combinations of patterns. Thus, a series of descending triangles would be considered a "plateau" or "resistance area." This is illustrated in Figure 8–9. Prices can also move out of a trading range on a "spike" as shown in Figure 8–6. This supposedly results from a sudden and dramatic change in the market environment. Spikes appear on charts as extreme rises or drops that make a dagger pattern. Spikes are often accompanied by limit moves on exchanges.

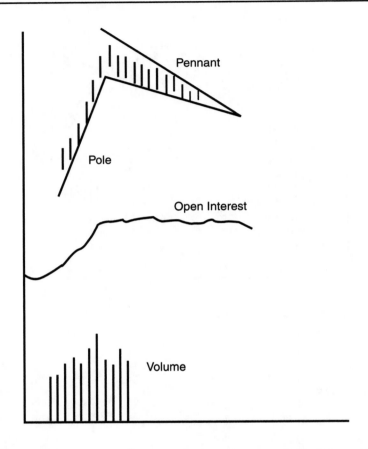

**Fig. 8–8** Pennant

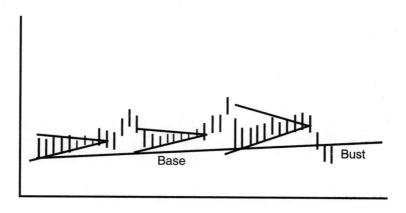

**Fig. 8–9** Descending Triangles

# History and Growth

Early attempts at introducing futures contracts on energy-related products were unsuccessful and were abandoned. However, the early failures have been followed by several highly successful energy futures contracts in both the United States and Europe. Futures contracts for the delivery of heating oil, unleaded gasoline, crude oil, natural gas, gas oil, Brent crude oil, and propane are very well established and have had an important impact on the pricing and distribution of those products. The success of these contracts encouraged the introduction of other energy-related futures contracts. The electricity futures contracts, which had such a brilliant start between 1996 and 1998, have recently experienced limited trading activity. Coal futures were introduced in 2001. In addition, options contracts on energy futures have increased the ability of smaller hedgers and speculators to participate in energy futures markets and it is expected that the introduction of new futures contracts in the coming years will further broaden the appeal and usefulness of energy futures markets.

Thus, the scope and importance of energy futures contracts should continue to grow in the future. However, it is by no means assured that all of those futures contracts will eventually be successful. Indeed, past experience suggests that the right combination of timing, luck, contract specifications, and market conditions is necessary for the success of a particular futures contract. Thus, prior to chronicling the development of energy futures contracts it is useful to review those factors that seem crucial to the success or failure of a futures contract.

# REQUIREMENTS FOR SUCCESS

In order to have a successful futures contract, three important factors must be present. First, the commodity must be homogeneous and fungible. Homogeneity is required because the futures market must have a standardized grade of the commodity to trade. The price of a particular futures contract will reflect the grade specified in the contract as satisfying the requirements for delivery. If delivery should occur, appropriate discounts and premiums from the price of the specified grade insure that delivery is convenient for a wide spectrum of market participants.

The ability to make and take delivery on a futures contract appears to be crucial to the early success of such contracts. Mature futures markets are primarily financial in nature and delivery occurs only rarely. However, in the initial stages of development of a futures contract, delivery is a much more common occurrence. Initially, market participants look at futures markets as another source of supply or as another outlet for the sale of unwanted product. At first, futures contracts are used only as forward pricing mechanisms. This is one of the most attractive features of futures markets to those who are unfamiliar with their operation. As markets mature, delivery occurs less frequently. A fully mature futures market will typically experience delivery on less than two percent of the contracts outstanding on a particular commodity.

The second requirement for a successful futures contract is that there must be significant hedger interest in the market. Firms that hold substantial cash market positions, or that may need to purchase or sell the commodity in the future, view price volatility as undesirable and use futures markets to reduce the risk of price changes in the cash market. The rationale for the existence of futures markets is that they provide a vehicle for the transfer of price risk from hedgers to speculators. Speculative interest alone is not sufficient to create a successful futures market.

Thus, for a futures contract to be successful there must be a large number of firms which can potentially use the futures contract in their operations. A cash market dominated by a few large firms would normally not be a candidate for a futures contract. Some participation on the part of speculators is also desirable. The existence of a large number of buyers and sellers in futures markets assures an adequate flow of buy and sell orders on the floor of the exchange and an efficient and competitive futures market pricing mechanism. Price manipulation is essentially impossible in organized futures markets.

The third requirement for a successful futures contract is that there must be price volatility. Prices must go down as well as up and the direction of change must be unpredictable. This is the same as saying that there must be price risk.

Price risk in futures markets attracts speculators who hope to profit from it. In general, the greater the price volatility the greater the potential profits to speculators. In addition, price volatility attracts hedgers who hope to use futures markets to eliminate price risk. If there is no price volatility then there is no need for hedgers to enter the market. Indeed, one of the most significant factors in the current success of energy futures contracts is the price volatility associated with the OPEC cartel and the resultant shortages and surpluses. The increased price volatility has attracted increased speculative interest in energy futures markets.

# COMMODITY EXCHANGES

As previously mentioned, commodity futures contracts are traded in centralized locations called commodity exchanges. The majority of the exchanges in the United States are not-for-profit membership associations with the exception of the New York Mercantile Exchange (NYMEX) and the Chicago Mercantile Exchange (CME) which have recently become for-profit corporations. Memberships are frequently bought and sold and membership entitles the owner of the seat to transact business on the floor of the exchange. The principal requirements for membership are good character and financial responsibility. Members of each exchange elect a board which is responsible for governing the conduct of members.

In the United States six commodity exchanges have traded energy-related futures contracts: the New York Mercantile Exchange (NYMEX); the Kansas City Board of Trade (KCBOT); the Chicago Board of Trade (CBOT); the Minneapolis Grain Exchange (MGE); the Chicago Mercantile Exchange (CME); and the New York Cotton Exchange (NYCE). In addition, the International Petroleum Exchange (IPE), the Singapore International Monetary Exchange (SIMEX), the Sydney Futures Exchange (SFE), and the New Zealand Futures Exchange (NZFE) have traded energy futures contracts.

# A SHORT HISTORY OF ENERGY FUTURES

Successful energy futures contracts are a recent phenomenon. Few people realize that the first energy futures contract was traded on a commodity exchange in the mid 1960s. This was the New York Cotton Exchange propane contract. Due to a lack of hedge participation and low price volatility, the contract was not successful and trading soon ceased.

In the early 1970s, after being turned down by several other commodity exchanges, Emmett Whitlock, a sugar futures trader, approached the New York Mercantile Exchange with a proposal to develop two futures contracts—gas oil and Bunker C oil—both with an ex-shore Rotterdam delivery of 100 metric tons. With the recommendation of NYMEX's president, Richard Levine, its Board of Governors reluctantly approved Whitlock's proposal, believing that NYMEX had "everything to gain and nothing to lose." NYMEX began trading its gas oil and Bunker C oil futures contracts in the fall of 1974. Coincidentally, around the same time, the New York Cotton Exchange opened trading in its crude oil futures contract, also with Rotterdam delivery.

The three contracts failed to attract much interest. One problem was that delivery was at a location remote from the trading point. Since it was difficult for business firms in the United States to take delivery in Rotterdam there was little hedging interest in the contracts. Further, during the 1974 oil embargo people were more concerned with being able to receive wet barrels than they were with hedging price risk. The New York Cotton Exchange allowed its crude oil contract to become dormant.

In spite of considerable skepticism in both the petroleum and futures industries, the New York Mercantile Exchange, under the leadership of Richard Levine, converted its Rotterdam delivery Bunker C oil futures contract to a No. 6 fuel oil futures contract with New York Harbor delivery. The Rotterdam gas oil futures contract was converted to a No. 2 heating oil futures contract, also with delivery in New York Harbor. On November 14, 1978, both contracts opened for trading.

The No. 6 fuel oil contract never attracted much attention. The major problem was that the contract specified delivery of a residual fuel oil with a very low sulfur content (.3%) consistent with New York City pollution laws. However, since a higher sulfur oil is allowed in much of the rest of the country, the No. 6 fuel oil futures contract was not useful outside of New York and thus was not successful. Only two contracts of No. 6 fuel oil were delivered through NYMEX—they were accepted by a local futures trader to heat his apartment building.

The No. 2 heating oil futures contract, however, was a different story. The initial skepticism was associated with the belief that the heating oil market was only a regional market and that prices only went up, never down. Heating oil prices were tied to the posted prices of the major oil companies and the spot market consisted of only the 100 or so largest independent firms connected by telephone and telex. Smaller firms had no access to the spot market and were limited to obtaining supplies from the major oil companies at contract posted prices.

The introduction of No. 2 heating oil futures trading allowed small jobbers and local distributors who had been excluded from spot market trading to get involved. This gave them another source of supply of product at prices not tied to the posted prices of the major oil companies. In addition, jobbers and distributors could sometimes sell excess supplies in futures markets at favorable prices. Use of the market by small jobbers and distributors was a major factor in the initial success of the heating oil futures contract.

The second oil crisis in 1979, caused by the fall of the Shah of Iran and the coming to power of the Ayatollah Khomeini, also contributed significantly to the popularity of the heating oil futures market. During the first few months of 1979, heating oil prices ran up from the low $.40s to the mid $.60s. Then, in June 1979, a second wave of price increases occurred when President Jimmy Carter enacted an entitlements program to encourage the movement of No. 2 heating oil to the northeastern United States. Prices climbed as high as $1.20 per gallon with the futures market locked limit up many days in a row before settling down to the $.70 per gallon price range at the end of the summer. Those firms which were participating in the futures market were able to advantageously hedge the enormous price movements in heating oil. Publicity concerning this successful use of the market encouraged many other firms to use the futures market as a device to hedge price risk. There is currently a much greater awareness on the part of the public and the oil industry of the usefulness and importance of the heating oil futures market. Volume and open interest have increased dramatically as the market has matured. The first delivery of heating oil in the futures market occurred in March 1979, and since then the NYMEX heating oil futures contract has facilitated the delivery of over 250 million barrels of heating oil, a dramatic success story.

It was the success of the New York Mercantile Exchange No. 2 heating oil futures contract which prompted other commodity exchanges to develop and introduce energy futures contracts. The introduction of new energy futures contracts has proceeded quite rapidly. The International Petroleum Exchange began trading a gas oil futures contract in the spring of 1981. The contract was immediately successful. The contract calls for delivery of gas oil, which is similar to heating oil, in the A.R.A. Area (Amsterdam, Rotterdam, and Antwerp).

The New York Mercantile Exchange began trading a futures contract for the delivery of leaded regular gasoline with New York Harbor delivery in

October 1981. Although the contract was highly successful, it was phased out when NYMEX began trading an unleaded regular gasoline contract with New York Harbor delivery in December 1984.

In the spring of 1983, NYMEX initiated a crude oil futures contract that calls for delivery of a "sweet" crude in Cushing, Oklahoma. Sweet crude is crude oil with a relatively low sulfur content. The crude oil futures contract is considered the most successful of the energy futures with daily trading volumes in excess of 100,000 contracts and open interest of over 450,000 contracts.

The Chicago Board of Trade started trading heating oil, gasoline, and crude oil futures contracts at the end of 1982 and the beginning of 1983. None of the contracts were successful because delivery on them required use of depository receipts, a method that was unacceptable to the petroleum industry. Similarly, the Chicago Mercantile Exchange began trading two energy futures contracts with Gulf Coast delivery which also did not succeed mainly because the petroleum industry could not relate to the minimum price fluctuations specified in the contracts.

The IPE launched a Brent crude oil futures contract in 1983. The contract, which required delivery by physicals, had limited success, and was revised in 1985 to a cash settlement delivery. The revised contract failed and Brent crude oil futures were reintroduced in 1988 with a cash settlement/EFP delivery. The new contract, with its innovative delivery method, was well received by the petroleum industry and grew rapidly.

On November 14, 1986, the eighth anniversary of its heating oil futures contract, NYMEX began trading its first options contract on crude oil futures. Because of the enormous volatility in the market, the options contract was very popular with both the petroleum and futures industries, and, in its first full year, more than three million contracts were traded. Heating oil options were introduced a year later, followed by unleaded gasoline options in 1989 and natural gas options in 1992. The options contracts added a new dimension to the energy futures markets.

In 1987, NYMEX started trading a propane futures contract. Although the contract has not lived up to expectations, trading only 40,000 to 50,000 contracts a year, it does have a consistent following and a growing demand for deliveries.

The Singapore International Monetary Exchange (SIMEX) launched a high sulfur fuel oil futures contract in 1989. The contract was initially successful, but because of changes in the spot market, participants left the futures market. Modifications made to the contract in 1998 have not revived interest.

In 1990, NYMEX began trading a Henry Hub natural gas futures contract. The contract was welcomed by the gas trading community and grew rapidly. On the other hand, two other natural gas futures contracts introduced by NYMEX in 1996, Permian Basin and Alberta, did not generate much interest and promptly failed.

In 1995, the Kansas City Board of Trade launched a competing natural gas futures contract requiring delivery of 10,000 MMBtus in the Permian Basin and WAHA Hub. The contract attracted only limited acceptance and became dormant in 1999.

Also in 1995, SIMEX introduced a Brent crude oil futures contract that offered a link-up with the IPE's contract. Through a mutual offset agreement between the two exchanges, Brent crude oil futures can be traded 18 hours a day.

In 1997, the IPE introduced a natural gas futures contract, its first non-oil contract, which is traded on its Energy Trading System (ETS).

With the expectation of deregulation of electricity, NYMEX inaugurated two electric futures contracts in 1996. On the other side of the world, the New Zealand Futures Exchange and the Sydney Futures Exchange introduced their own electricity futures contracts. From 1998 through 2001, eight more electric futures contracts were launched—four at NYMEX, two at the Chicago Board of Trade, one at the Minneapolis Grain Exchange, and one at the IPE. All the electric futures contracts have had limited trading activity.

## CURRENT STATUS OF ENERGY FUTURES CONTRACTS

Table 9–1 summarizes the most important features, specifications, and the status of all past and present futures contracts. Over the years, more than 52 energy futures contracts have been introduced by 10 commodity exchanges world-wide. Although most of the contracts listed are currently dormant, the exchanges are continually developing new energy contracts to trade. The most important futures contracts currently traded in terms of open interest may be ranked as follows:

| Exchange | Contract | Representative Open Interest |
|---|---|---|
| NYMEX | Crude Oil | 450,000 |
| NYMEX | Natural Gas | 350,000 |
| IPE | Crude Oil | 250,000 |
| NYMEX | Heating Oil | 125,000 |
| IPE | Gas Oil | 100,000 |
| NYMEX | Unleaded Gasoline | 100,000 |

| Contract | Exchange* | Initiation of Trading | Present Status | Size | Delivery Method |
|---|---|---|---|---|---|
| Crude Oil (Rotterdam) | NYCE | Sept 1974 | Dormant | 5,000 bbl | Physicals |
| Gas Oil (Rotterdam – ex-shore) | NYMEX | Oct 1974 | Dormant | 100 metric tons | Physicals |
| Bunker C Oil (Rotterdam – ex-shore) | NYMEX | Oct 1974 | Dormant | 100 metric tons | Physicals |
| No. 2 Heating Oil (New York Harbor) | NYMEX | Nov 1978 | ACTIVE | 42,000 gal | Physicals |
| No. 6 Fuel Oil (New York Harbor) | NYMEX | Nov 1978 | Dormant | 42,000 gal | Physicals |
| Gas Oil (A.R.A. Area) | IPE | Apr 1981 Revised 1984 | ACTIVE | 100 metric tons | Warrants (1981) Physicals (1984) |
| No. 2 Heating Oil (Gulf Coast) | NYMEX | Aug 1981 | Dormant | 42,000 gal | Physicals |
| Leaded Regular Gasoline (New York Harbor) | NYMEX | Oct 1981 | Dormant | 42,000 gal | Physicals |
| Leaded Regular Gasoline (Gulf Coast) | NYMEX | Dec 1981 | Dormant | 42,000 gal | Physicals |

**Table 9–1** Past and Present Energy Futures Contracts

| Contract | Exchange* | Initiation of Trading | Present Status | Size | Delivery Method |
|---|---|---|---|---|---|
| Propane (Mont Belvieu, TX) | NYCE | Dec 1981 (Revised) | Dormant | 42,000 gal | Shipping Certificates |
| Unleaded Regular Gasoline (Gulf Coast) | CBOT | Dec 1982 | Dormant | 42,000 gal | Depository Receipts |
| Crude Oil (Cushing, OK) | NYMEX | Mar 1983 | ACTIVE | 1,000 bbl | Physicals |
| Crude Oil (St. James, LA) | CBOT | Mar 1983 | Dormant | 1,000 bbl | Depository Receipts |
| No. 2 Heating Oil (Gulf Coast) | CBOT | Apr 1983 | Dormant | 42,000 gal | Depository Receipts |
| Crude Oil (1983) (Brent) | IPE | Nov 1983 Revised 1985 Revised 1988 | ACTIVE | 1,000 bbl | Physicals (1983) Cash Settlement (1985) Cash Settlement/EFP (1988) |
| Leaded Regular Gasoline (Gulf Coast) | CME | Mar 1984 | Dormant | 42,000 gal | Physicals |
| No. 2 Heating Oil (Gulf Coast) | CME | Mar 1984 | Dormant | 42,000 gal | Physicals |

**Table 9–1 (cont.)** Past and Present Energy Futures Contracts

| Contract | Exchange* | Initiation of Trading | Present Status | Size | Delivery Method |
|---|---|---|---|---|---|
| Unleaded Regular Gasoline (New York Harbor) | NYMEX | Dec 1984 | ACTIVE | 42,000 gal | Physicals |
| Heavy Fuel Oil (A.R.A. Area) | IPE | Oct 1986 Revised 1987 Revised 1989 | Dormant | 100 metric tons | Physicals (1986) Physicals (1987) Cash Settlement (1989) |
| Propane (Mont Belvieu, TX) | NYMEX | Aug 1987 | ACTIVE | 42,000 gal | Physicals |
| High Sulfur Fuel Oil (Singapore Port) | SIMEX | Feb 1989 Revised 1998 | Dormant | 100 metric tons | Physicals/Cash Settlement |
| Residual Fuel Oil (New York Harbor) | NYMEX | Oct 1989 | Dormant | 42,000 gal | Physicals |
| Natural Gas (Henry Hub) | NYMEX | Apr 1990 | ACTIVE | 10,000 MMBtu | Physicals |
| Crude Oil (Dubai) | SIMEX | June 1990 | Dormant | 1,000 bbl | Cash Settlement |
| Crude Oil (Dubai) | IPE | July 1990 | Dormant | 1,000 bbl | Cash Settlement |

**Table 9–1 (cont.)** Past and Present Energy Futures Contracts

| Contract | Exchange* | Initiation of Trading | Present Status | Size | Delivery Method |
|---|---|---|---|---|---|
| Naphtha (A.R.A. Area) | IPE | Apr 1991 | Dormant | 100 metric tons | Physicals |
| Gas Oil (Singapore) | SIMEX | June 1991 | Dormant | 100 metric tons | Physicals |
| Unleaded Gasoline (A.R.A. Area) | IPE | Jan 1992 | Dormant | 100 metric tons | Physicals |
| Sour Crude Oil (Texas) | NYMEX | Feb 1992 | Dormant | 1,000 bbl | Physicals |
| Unleaded Gasoline. (Gulf Coast) | NYMEX | Sept 1992 | Dormant | 42,000 gal | Physicals |
| Crude Oil (Brent) | SIMEX | June 1995 | Dormant | 1,000 bbl | Cash Settlement/EFP |
| Natural Gas (Permian/WAHA Hub) | KCBOT | Aug 1995 | Dormant | 10,000 MMBtu | Physicals |
| Electricity (Palo Verde) | NYMEX | Mar 1996 Revised 1998 | Dormant | 736 Mwh 864 Mwh 432 Mwh | Physicals Physicals Physicals |

**Table 9–1 (cont.)** Past and Present Energy Futures Contracts

| Contract | Exchange* | Initiation of Trading | Present Status | Size | Delivery Method |
|---|---|---|---|---|---|
| Electricity (California–Oregon Border) | NYMEX | Mar 1996 Revised 1998 | Dormant | 736 Mwh 864 Mwh 432 Mwh | Physicals Physicals Physicals |
| Natural Gas (Permian Basin) | NYMEX | May 1996 | Dormant | 10,000 MMBtu | Physicals |
| Natural Gas (Alberta) | NYMEX | Sept 1996 | Dormant | 10,000 MMBtu | Physicals |
| Electricity (New Zealand) | NZFE | Nov 1996 | Dormant | 250 Mwh | Cash Settlement |
| Natural Gas (UK NBP) | IPE | Jan 1997 | ACTIVE | 1,000 therms (Trading unit: 5,000 therms) | Physicals |
| Electricity (New South Wales, Australia) | SFE | Sept 1997 | Dormant | 500 Mwh | Cash Settlement |
| Electricity (Victoria, Australia) | SFE | Sept 1997 | Dormant | 500 Mwh | Cash Settlement |
| Electricity (Cinergy) | NYMEX | July 1998 | Dormant | 736 Mwh | Physicals |

**Table 9–1 (cont.)** Past and Present Energy Futures Contracts

| Contract | Exchange* | Initiation of Trading | Present Status | Size | Delivery Method |
|---|---|---|---|---|---|
| Electricity (Entergy) | NYMEX | July 1998 | Dormant | 736 Mwh | Physicals |
| Electricity (TVA) | CBOT | Sept 1998 | Dormant | 1,680 Mwh | Physicals |
| Electricity (ComEd) | CBOT | Sept 1998 | Dormant | 1,680 Mwh | Physicals |
| Electricity (Twin Cities) | MGE | Sept 1998 | Dormant | 736 Mwh | Physicals |
| Fuel Oil (A.R.A. Area) | IPE | Mar 1999 | Dormant | 100 metric tons | Physicals |
| Electricity (Pennsylvania, New Jersey, Maryland) | NYMEX | Mar 1999 | Dormant | 736 Mwh | Physicals |
| Crude Oil (Middle East Sour) | NYMEX | May 2000 | Dormant | 1,000 bbl | Cash Settlement/EFP |
| Electricity (Mid-Columbia) | NYMEX | Jan 2001 | Dormant | 432 Mwh | Physicals |

**Table 9–1 (cont.)** Past and Present Energy Futures Contracts

| Contract | Exchange* | Initiation of Trading | Present Status | Size | Delivery Method |
|---|---|---|---|---|---|
| Electricity (Energy Account) | IPE | Mar 2001 | ACTIVE | 720 Mwh (Trading Unit: Multiples of 5) | Physicals |
| Coal (CAPP) (Central Appalachia) | NYMEX | July 2001 | ACTIVE | 1,550 tons | Physicals |
| Crude Oil (Brent) | NYMEX | Sept 2001 | ACTIVE | 1,000 bbl | Cash Settlement/EFP |

**\*Exchanges**

| | |
|---|---|
| NYMEX | New York Mercantile Exchange |
| NYCE | New York Cotton Exchange (now known as New York Board of Trade) |
| CME | Chicago Mercantile Exchange |
| KCBOT | Kansas City Board of Trade |
| NZFE | New Zealand Futures Exchange |
| IPE | International Petroleum Exchange |
| CBOT | Chicago Board of Trade |
| SIMEX | Singapore International Monetary Exchange |
| SFE | Sydney Futures Exchange |
| MGE | Minneapolis Grain Exchange |

Note: Although all the electric futures contracts are listed as dormant, some of the commodity exchanges are actively promoting their contracts in anticipation of future trading activity.

**Table 9–1 (cont.)** Past and Present Energy Futures Contracts

Table 9–2 shows the growth in volume of NYMEX's No. 2 heating oil futures contract from its inception in 1978 through 2000. The heating oil futures contract was the first successful energy futures contract in the world. Its success encouraged NYMEX to expand its energy futures markets to include leaded gasoline futures, in 1981, and crude oil futures, in 1983. The heating oil market is seasonal in nature with peak demand occurring in the winter months. Thus, the futures market flourished in 1980, its second full year of operation, because market participants had two full seasons of experience with futures markets. The continued growth of deliveries, open interest, and trading volume over the last 20 years is a sign of a healthy and expanding futures market.

| Year | Futures Trading Volume | Futures Open Interest | Options Trading Volume | Deliveries |
|---|---|---|---|---|
| 1978 | 116 | 535 | — | 0 |
| 1979 | 33,804 | 1,973 | — | 810 |
| 1980 | 238,284 | 11,556 | — | 4,799 |
| 1981 | 995,506 | 31,585 | — | 15,577 |
| 1982 | 1,743,526 | 21,848 | — | 17,009 |
| 1983 | 1,868,322 | 30,916 | — | 9,870 |
| 1984 | 2,091,546 | 25,371 | — | 14,061 |
| 1985 | 2,207,733 | 31,172 | — | 11,020 |
| 1986 | 3,275,044 | 72,564 | — | 12,239 |
| 1987 | 4,293,395 | 63,427 | 143,605 | 10,440 |
| 1988 | 4,935,015 | 74,797 | 125,812 | 12,014 |
| 1989 | 5,740,967 | 97,947 | 298,136 | 11,666 |
| 1990 | 6,376,871 | 72,444 | 406,810 | 11,105 |
| 1991 | 6,680,171 | 113,559 | 709,053 | 11,789 |
| 1992 | 8,005,462 | 130,832 | 1,247,891 | 17,082 |
| 1993 | 8,625,061 | 185,425 | 803,216 | 16,618 |
| 1994 | 8,986,835 | 132,743 | 699,325 | 15,218 |
| 1995 | 8,266,783 | 128,834 | 703,388 | 14,948 |
| 1996 | 8,341,877 | 95,408 | 1,108,935 | 22,141 |
| 1997 | 8,370,964 | 152,476 | 1,147,034 | 29,816 |
| 1998 | 8,863,764 | 176,361 | 669,725 | 30,592 |
| 1999 | 9,200,703 | 135,259 | 695,558 | 15,397 |
| 2000 | 9,631,376 | 124,664 | 1,385,968 | 28,708 |

**Table 9–2** Growth of New York Mercantile Exchange No. 2 Heating Oil Futures and Options Contracts

Table 9–3 shows the growth of NYMEX's unleaded gasoline futures market. Although the unleaded gasoline futures contract began trading in December 1984, it has its roots in the leaded gasoline futures contract which began trading three years earlier but was phased out as the United States switched from leaded to unleaded gasoline. Thus, the unleaded gasoline futures contract could be considered NYMEX's second oldest energy futures contract. Despite the constant contract specification changes required as the EPA, the 50 states, and the oil industry determine the best gasoline for our environment, the unleaded gasoline futures market continues to grow. Similar to the heating oil futures contract, the open interest in the unleaded gasoline futures contract seemed to jump dramatically just prior to the second heavy buying period, the spring driving period.

| Year | Futures Trading Volume | Futures Open Interest | Options Trading Volume | Deliveries |
|------|------|------|------|------|
| 1985 | 132,611 | 3,150 | — | 4,343 |
| 1986 | 439,352 | 27,100 | — | 4,988 |
| 1987 | 2,056,238 | 38,968 | — | 12,667 |
| 1988 | 3,292,055 | 47,189 | — | 10,994 |
| 1989 | 4,484,558 | 69,394 | 332,094 | 15,539 |
| 1990 | 5,205,995 | 53,328 | 435,685 | 12,128 |
| 1991 | 5,509,926 | 123,103 | 521,734 | 10,824 |
| 1992 | 6,674,757 | 71,833 | 860,086 | 11,228 |
| 1993 | 7,407,809 | 137,165 | 660,886 | 13,370 |
| 1994 | 7,470,836 | 53,203 | 573,502 | 16,821 |
| 1995 | 7,071,787 | 61,632 | 766,557 | 8,591 |
| 1996 | 6,312,339 | 59,806 | 655,965 | 12,318 |
| 1997 | 7,475,145 | 100,742 | 1,033,778 | 12,637 |
| 1998 | 7,992,269 | 100,465 | 730,421 | 18,080 |
| 1999 | 8,701,216 | 89,804 | 600,009 | 19,774 |
| 2000 | 8,645,182 | 90,242 | 1,012,460 | 21,003 |

**Table 9–3** Growth of New York Mercantile Exchange Unleaded Gasoline Futures and Options Contracts

The spectacular growth of NYMEX's crude oil futures contract is shown in Table 9–4. As in the heating oil and unleaded gasoline futures contracts, the crude oil futures contract's growth exploded after its second year of trading to become the largest energy futures contract in the world. To encourage new participants to trade its futures contracts, NYMEX has over the years expanded the deliverable grades of crude to include six domestic grades (West Texas Intermediate, Low Sweet Mix, New Mexican Sweet, North Texas Sweet, Oklahoma Sweet, and South Texas Sweet) and six foreign grades (U.K. Brent, Norwegian Oseberg Blend, U.K. Forties, Nigerian Light, Colombian Cusiana, and Qua Iboe). Some of the foreign crudes are deliverable at a discount or at a premium or at par. NYMEX has also expanded the trading months to seven years in the future which allows hedgers to lock in profit margins years in advance. The growth of the open interest to nearly half a million contracts shows the continued success of the crude oil futures market.

| Year | Futures Trading Volume | Futures Open Interest | Options Trading Volume | Deliveries |
|------|------|------|------|------|
| 1983 | 323,153 | 21,554 | — | 1,619 |
| 1984 | 1,840,342 | 49,201 | — | 17,265 |
| 1985 | 3,980,867 | 60,757 | — | 25,829 |
| 1986 | 8,313,529 | 121,248 | 135,266 | 20,551 |
| 1987 | 14,581,614 | 208,259 | 3,117,037 | 16,697 |
| 1988 | 18,858,948 | 185,218 | 5,480,281 | 9,137 |
| 1989 | 20,534,865 | 250,117 | 5,685,953 | 15,283 |
| 1990 | 23,686,897 | 219,473 | 5,254,612 | 18,832 |
| 1991 | 21,005,867 | 285,921 | 4,416,126 | 16,755 |
| 1992 | 21,109,562 | 331,827 | 6,562,163 | 18,548 |
| 1993 | 24,868,602 | 412,117 | 7,156,518 | 30,161 |
| 1994 | 26,812,262 | 354,416 | 5,675,072 | 27,711 |
| 1995 | 23,613,994 | 353,354 | 3,975,611 | 35,213 |
| 1996 | 23,487,821 | 364,170 | 5,271,456 | 18,739 |
| 1997 | 24,771,375 | 413,045 | 5,079,607 | 25,832 |
| 1998 | 30,495,647 | 483,327 | 7,448,095 | 23,754 |
| 1999 | 37,860,064 | 501,819 | 8,161,976 | 38,655 |
| 2000 | 36,882,692 | 407,646 | 7,460,052 | 8,316 |

**Table 9–4** Growth of New York Mercantile Exchange Crude Oil Futures and Options Contracts (Cushing, Oklahoma)

The NYMEX natural gas futures contract, which began trading in 1990, is now the second largest energy futures market in the world. Its rapid growth, as shown in Table 9–5, has surprised both the energy and futures communities. The contract calls for delivery of 10,000 MMBtus in the Henry Hub area. NYMEX also introduced two additional natural gas contracts, one requiring delivery in Alberta, the other in the Permian Basin. Unfortunately these two contracts failed to attract a sufficient number of hedgers and speculators to make them successful, and they were delisted. The Henry Hub contract, on the other hand, became so widely accepted that it generated a significant EFP market to allow hedgers to protect both prices and supplies anywhere in the United States and Canada.

| Year | Futures Trading Volume | Futures Open Interest | Options Trading Volume | Deliveries |
|------|------|------|------|------|
| 1990 | 132,820 | 9,064 | — | 917 |
| 1991 | 418,410 | 18,352 | — | 2,719 |
| 1992 | 1,920,986 | 68,809 | 80,756 | 6,919 |
| 1993 | 4,671,533 | 126,160 | 345,814 | 10,417 |
| 1994 | 6,357,560 | 133,834 | 493,491 | 15,923 |
| 1995 | 8,086,718 | 162,783 | 921,520 | 20,025 |
| 1996 | 8,813,867 | 143,846 | 1,234,691 | 30,168 |
| 1997 | 11,923,628 | 186,815 | 2,079,607 | 38,794 |
| 1998 | 15,978,286 | 222,576 | 3,115,765 | 44,848 |
| 1999 | 19,165,096 | 246,629 | 3,849,454 | 42,732 |
| 2000 | 17,875,013 | 353,093 | 5,335,800 | 32,445 |

**Table 9–5** Growth of New York Mercantile Exchange Natural Gas Futures and Options Contracts

The International Petroleum Exchange (IPE) was established in 1980 to provide a marketplace for trading energy futures in London. Its first contract, introduced in 1981, was gas oil futures. Initially, the contract called for delivery of 100 metric tons in the Antwerp, Rotterdam, Amsterdam Area by use of warrants. In 1984, on the recommendation of the oil industry, the contract was revised to require a physical delivery. Table 9–6 shows the growth in futures trading volume and open interest of the IPE's gas oil futures contract. Gas oil options were introduced in 1988.

| Year | Futures Trading Volume | Futures Open Interest | Options Trading Volume |
|---|---|---|---|
| 1981 | 149,722 | N/A* | — |
| 1982 | 623,308 | N/A | — |
| 1983 | 608,529 | N/A | — |
| 1984 | 535,495 | N/A | — |
| 1985 | 509,886 | N/A | — |
| 1986 | 938,226 | N/A | — |
| 1987 | 1,102,148 | N/A | 7,518 |
| 1988 | 1,556,958 | N/A | 16,246 |
| 1989 | 1,957,356 | 45,804 | 35,045 |
| 1990 | 2,603,095 | 45,956 | 101,963 |
| 1991 | 2,854,961 | 60,723 | 91,089 |
| 1992 | 3,452,643 | 70,104 | 199,256 |
| 1993 | 3,608,637 | 110,083 | 217,058 |
| 1994 | 3,779,064 | 98,857 | 136,859 |
| 1995 | 4,491,463 | 72,670 | 116,424 |
| 1996 | 4,361,062 | 86,733 | 110,226 |
| 1997 | 4,031,608 | 91,346 | 68,195 |
| 1998 | 4,962,838 | 139,201 | 104,133 |
| 1999 | 6,150,912 | 118,648 | 104,813 |
| 2000 | 7,115,435 | 91,354 | 100,631 |

*Statistics not available

**Table 9–6** Growth of International Petroleum Exchange Gas Oil Futures and Options Contracts

The IPE launched a Brent crude oil futures contract, its second energy futures contract, in 1983. The contract, which required the physical delivery of 1,000 barrels of oil, was received with mixed results and was subsequently modified in 1985 by substituting a cash settlement for the physical delivery mechanism. The contract was further modified in 1988 to allow for Exchange for Physicals (EFPs) as well as cash settlement. Since 1988, the Brent crude oil futures contract has grown rapidly in both trading volume and open interest, as shown in Table 9–7, to become the world's third largest energy futures contract.

| Year | Futures Trading Volume | Futures Open Interest | Options Trading Volume |
|------|------------------------|-----------------------|------------------------|
| 1988 | 29,823 | N/A* | — |
| 1989 | 1,671,786 | 31,752 | 60,589 |
| 1990 | 4,083,092 | 50,623 | 153,278 |
| 1991 | 5,230,892 | 72,370 | 232,118 |
| 1992 | 6,172,156 | 88,687 | 791,810 |
| 1993 | 8,852,549 | 140,552 | 1,059,222 |
| 1994 | 10,082,761 | 158,715 | 531,742 |
| 1995 | 9,773,146 | 161,235 | 571,308 |
| 1996 | 10,675,389 | 140,504 | 374,233 |
| 1997 | 10,301,918 | 189,672 | 250,176 |
| 1998 | 13,623,789 | 245,099 | 334,977 |
| 1999 | 15,982,337 | 241,548 | 495,798 |
| 2000 | 17,297,974 | 303,063 | 452,284 |

*Statistics not available

**Table 9–7** Growth of International Petroleum Exchange Crude Oil Futures and Options Contracts

Table 9–8 shows the pattern of delivery versus volume on the NYMEX No. 2 heating oil futures contract. Initially, deliveries constituted about 5 or 6% of cumulative contract volume. However, this percentage figure has decreased steadily over the years so that currently less than 1% of contract volume is typically delivered. This steady reduction in deliveries indicates an increase in maturation of the heating oil futures market and an increasing sophistication on the part of market participants. Also, the fact that there is a close price correlation between the futures settlement price on the last day of trading and New York Harbor spot prices shows the financial hedge advantage of the futures market. Thus, the heating oil futures market is currently a financial market where delivery is quite rare.

| Year | Number of Deliveries | Cumulative Futures Volume | Deliveries as a % of Volume |
|------|------|------|------|
| 1979 | 810 | 11,787 | 6.87 |
| 1980 | 4,799 | 115,136 | 4.17 |
| 1981 | 15,577 | 811,448 | 1,92 |
| 1982 | 17,009 | 1,672,179 | 1.02 |
| 1983 | 9,870 | 1,844,250 | 0.53 |
| 1984 | 14,061 | 2,117,019 | 0.61 |
| 1985 | 11,020 | 2,069,901 | 0.53 |
| 1986 | 12,239 | 3,034,981 | 0.40 |
| 1987 | 10,440 | 4,021,241 | 0.26 |
| 1988 | 12,014 | 4,923,343 | 0.24 |
| 1989 | 11,666 | 5,243,235 | 0.22 |
| 1990 | 11,105 | 6,692,951 | 0.17 |
| 1991 | 11,789 | 6,091,152 | 0.19 |
| 1992 | 17,082 | 7,800,442 | 0.22 |
| 1993 | 16,618 | 8,439,375 | 0.20 |
| 1994 | 15,218 | 9,183,276 | 0.17 |
| 1995 | 14,948 | 8,168,203 | 0.18 |
| 1996 | 22,141 | 8,503,579 | 0.26 |
| 1997 | 29,816 | 8,668,074 | 0.34 |
| 1998 | 30,592 | 8,518,727 | 0.36 |
| 1999 | 15,397 | 9,379,616 | 0.16 |
| 2000 | 28,708 | 9,767,554 | 0.29 |

**Table 9–8** New York Mercantile Exchange—Deliveries on the No. 2 Heating Oil Futures Contract

In March 1996, NYMEX inaugurated the first two electricity contracts—California-Oregon Border and Palo Verde. Both contracts required the physical delivery of electricity over a prescribed period of time. Electricity futures contracts using the cash settlement delivery method have since been introduced in New Zealand and Australia. In 1998, the Chicago Board of Trade began trading TVA and ComEd electric futures contracts; the Minneapolis Grain Exchange started a Twin Cities electric futures contract; and NYMEX introduced three additional electric futures contracts—Cinergy, Entergy, and PJM, all of which require physical delivery.

| Contract Month | California–Oregon Border Electricity Futures Contract | | | Palo Verde Electricity Futures Contract | | |
|---|---|---|---|---|---|---|
| | Deliveries | Cumulative Futures Volume | Deliveries as a % of Volume | Deliveries | Cumulative Futures Volume | Deliveries as a % of Volume |
| June 1996 | 30 | 7,115 | 0.42 | 95 | 1,235 | 7.69 |
| July | 118 | 6,173 | 1.91 | 172 | 1,068 | 16.10 |
| Aug | 165 | 4,851 | 3.40 | 95 | 1,167 | 8.14 |
| Sep | 50 | 4,260 | 1.17 | 30 | 1,711 | 1.75 |
| Oct | 87 | 3,034 | 2.87 | 75 | 1,459 | 5.14 |
| Nov | 14 | 3,798 | 0.74 | 150 | 1,869 | 8.03 |
| Dec | 195 | 5,164 | 3.78 | 306 | 1,956 | 15.64 |
| Jan 1997 | 278 | 8,431 | 3.30 | 348 | 3,260 | 10.67 |
| Feb | 212 | 5,513 | 3.85 | 98 | 3,096 | 3.17 |
| Mar | 100 | 3,029 | 3.30 | 99 | 2,068 | 4.79 |
| Apr | 168 | 3,269 | 5.14 | 50 | 3,122 | 1.60 |
| May | 225 | 5,646 | 3.99 | 230 | 4,363 | 5.27 |
| June | 519 | 7,948 | 6.53 | 260 | 7,948 | 3.27 |
| July | 190 | 11,278 | 1.68 | 362 | 14,270 | 2.54 |
| Aug | 137 | 11,355 | 1.21 | 346 | 18,387 | 1.88 |

**Table 9–9** New York Mercantile Exchange Electricity Futures Deliveries

| Contract Month | California–Oregon Border Electricity Futures Contract | | | Palo Verde Electricity Futures Contract | | |
|---|---|---|---|---|---|---|
| | Deliveries | Cumulative Futures Volume | Deliveries as a % of Volume | Deliveries | Cumulative Futures Volume | Deliveries as a % of Volume |
| Sep | 255 | 11,315 | 2.25 | 325 | 21,621 | 1.50 |
| Oct | 125 | 9,652 | 1.30 | 362 | 20,643 | 1.75 |
| Nov | 250 | 10,119 | 2.47 | 285 | 27,177 | 1.05 |
| Dec | 375 | 15,569 | 2.41 | 356 | 17,124 | 2.08 |
| Jan 1998 | 397 | 11,899 | 3.34 | 362 | 12,127 | 2.99 |
| Feb | 75 | 10,077 | 0.74 | 154 | 9,324 | 1.65 |
| Mar | 56 | 10,048 | 0.56 | 321 | 10,686 | 3.00 |
| Apr | 45 | 11,156 | 0.40 | 75 | 11,356 | 0.66 |
| May | 263 | 11,859 | 2.22 | 157 | 12,798 | 1.23 |
| June | 175 | 14,920 | 1.17 | 538 | 19,891 | 2.70 |
| July | 189 | 15,592 | 1.21 | 329 | 22,809 | 1.44 |
| Aug | 125 | 19,573 | 0.64 | 250 | 21,799 | 1.15 |
| Sep | 250 | 16,983 | 1.50 | 511 | 22,158 | 2.30 |
| Oct | 29 | 7,176 | 0.40 | 243 | 7,222 | 3.40 |
| Nov | 85 | 6,930 | 1.23 | 103 | 5,231 | 1.97 |

**Table 9–9 (cont.)** New York Mercantile Exchange Electricity Futures Deliveries

The success or failure of each of these contracts will be determined by the number of hedgers who embrace the market as well as the ease of completing the physical transfer of electricity through its respective grid. Table 9–9 shows the initial growth of deliveries and the relationship between the number and deliveries and cumulative futures trading volume of NYMEX's original two electric futures contracts. Both contracts exhibit steadily declining delivery versus volume percentages, similar to those exhibited by NYMEX's No. 2 heating oil futures contract (shown in Table 9–8), which is usually a sign of a healthy and growing market.

The summer of 1998, however, was a difficult period for the electric community. A rapid rise in the demand for electricity caused a spiraling of wholesale prices. After it was over, a number of companies filed for bankruptcy protection while others re-evaluated their roles in the electric cash market. Although the obligations of buyers and sellers in the futures market were met, reduced participation of locals and speculators caused a lack of liquidity in the market. Locals and speculators were unable to limit or transfer price risk of their short positions by either spreading into other contract months or other contracts. The cash market also suffered liquidity problems as it was converted into a dealers' market.

The commodity exchanges have not given up on electric futures; rather, they are waiting for a more opportune time to reintroduce the contracts when physical transfers of electricity can be completed at a reasonable cost across the various grid systems.

# DELIVERY METHODS

The delivery mechanism is one of the most important features of a particular futures contract and is often a crucial determinant of its success or failure. Because of the high percentage of deliveries during the initial stages of futures markets, the ease and clarity of the delivery mechanism is important in encouraging hedge participation. In energy futures a number of different delivery methods are possible, as illustrated in Table 9–1.

The most common delivery method is to deliver the physicals (wet barrels). This corresponds to common commercial practice and is readily understood by potential market participants. Delivery occurs at a designated place and product is transferred into the buyer's truck, barge, tanker, or pipeline. It has the advantage of not tying up storage facilities. The seller merely notifies the clearing member of the intention to deliver at a particular approved facility at a particular time. The buyer is then notified of that time and the place of delivery. The method has the disadvantage that it requires a lot of coordination on the part of the clearing members to match up buyers and sellers and to insure that delivery does indeed occur. Currently, delivery of physicals is the most common mechanism. It is used in NYMEX heating oil, gasoline, crude oil, natural gas, propane, and electricity contracts.

The International Petroleum Exchange (IPE) used warrants to deliver on its gas oil contract until April 1985 when the IPE transferred to physical (wet barrel) delivery similar to NYMEX contracts. The warrant mechanism is very similar to warehouse receipts commonly used in the United States. The seller places product in a certified storage facility and the facility issues the warrant. The seller then delivers the warrant in satisfaction of the obligation on the futures contract. This method has the advantage of ease of delivery. The disadvantage is that it requires a large number of certified storage facilities and there are potential problems if storage in relation to open interest is too low.

The New York Cotton Exchange (now known as the New York Board of Trade) used a shipping certificate method of delivery on its propane contract. Propane was stored in large salt domes in Mont Belvieu, Texas, and Conway, Kansas. The seller obtained shipping certificates against propane stored in these salt domes and passed the certificates to the clearing member. The buyer had 30 days to lift the propane and take delivery. The shipping certificate guaranteed that there was product in the storage facility and allowed for the expeditious collection of funds by the seller. The method worked well because there were large storage facilities available. The exchange terminated its propane contract in the mid 1980s due to a lack of volume and to allow it to be reintroduced on NYMEX with a physical delivery mechanism.

Certificate delivery was an innovation of the Chicago Board of Trade and was used for delivery on its heating oil and gasoline contracts. This method required that the seller obtain a depository receipt from an issuer approved by the exchange. Depository receipts were issued by approved oil firms, which had access to the three major pipelines in the Gulf Coast area. The CBOT gasoline and heating oil futures contracts called for Gulf Coast delivery. Few firms applied for permission to issue depository receipts and this may have been the main reason for the failure of the CBOT heating oil and gasoline futures contracts.

Cash settlement is the newest delivery method whereby the exchange or clearinghouse gathers published prices of the commodity over a predetermined period of time and averages the prices into one cash settlement price. All open futures positions after the last trading day are marked to the cash settlement price and liquidated. Cash settlement is advantageous because it offers a simple means of settling up responsibilities of both the buyer and the seller who need only transfer money through the exchange's clearinghouse with neither party to the transaction making direct contact with the other party. The disadvantages are the possible manipulation of cash prices and the inability of a buyer to secure physicals at a comparable price or a seller's inability to dispose of physicals at a comparable price.

To circumvent the disadvantages of cash settlement, some futures contracts are designed with an EFP (Exchange of Futures for Physicals or Exchange for Product) mechanism which allows a firm with a long or short position in the market, after the termination of trading, to locate a firm with an opposite position of equal size. The two firms are matched—a transfer of physicals takes place between them and their futures positions are liquidated at a mutually agreed upon cash price prior to the exchange's liquidation of all open futures positions at the cash settlement price.

The IPE has developed an effective cash settlement/EFP delivery mechanism for its Brent crude oil futures contract (see Appendix H). The same mechanism is used for SIMEX's Brent crude oil futures contract that is an offshoot of the IPE contract.

# NEW FUTURES CONTRACTS

The increased volatility of energy prices associated with shortages or surpluses and the actions of the OPEC cartel are important factors in the continued development of futures contracts on energy-related products. As a result of continued deregulation of electricity, NYMEX began trading a Mid-Columbia electric futures contract in January 2001 and the IPE introduced an electricity (energy account) contract in March 2001. In August 2001 a coal futures contract for Central Appalachia was launched on NYMEX. In addition, NYMEX in September 2001 introduced a Brent crude futures contract with a cash settlement/EFP delivery method in direct competition with the IPE.

# 10

# Economic Implications of Energy Futures and Options

## BENEFITS OF ENERGY FUTURES AND OPTIONS MARKETS

Energy futures and options contracts and markets provide many benefits to market participants and the public at large. One of the most important benefits is a highly visible and efficient price discovery mechanism. Futures contracts trade under conditions that closely approximate perfect competition; there are a large number of buyers and sellers conducting transactions in a homogenous product. Exchange rules prevent manipulation and ensure fair, open, and honest trading. In addition, there is an efficient and essentially costless information system, and except for financial responsibility there are no barriers to entry into the market. Under such conditions the price which results can be considered to be the "proper" price in the sense that it represents the consensus results of the decisions of many thousands of independent market participants.

Prior to the advent of energy futures markets there was no visible, widely quoted benchmark price. Often those prices quoted were subject to modifications and discounts which rendered them useless in making decisions. OPEC-posted prices were often subject to political as well as supply and demand considerations. Different major oil companies would often sell product to their customers at substantially different prices. In addition, the cash energy prices quoted in one market are usually not representative of prices in other geographic locations.

Futures prices are not subject to the problems of posted and spot market prices. Futures prices are determined in a central marketplace and are representative of standardized quantities and qualities of petroleum product trading at a particular location (the delivery point of the contract). Cash prices of product of different quality may be established by using this benchmark price plus or minus an appropriate quality differential. Similarly, the benchmark may be used to establish cash prices in different locations with the use of transportation differentials. This objective benchmark information is useful even for those who are not participating in the cash market. Futures quotes are available worldwide on a daily basis in newspapers and instantaneously via electronic media.

The relationship between cash and futures prices provides useful signals to cash market participants in their decision to buy, sell, and store product. An inverted market, for instance, provides a signal to inventory holders that it is more profitable to sell product immediately and thus avoid storage costs. When product is sold, the firm desiring to own product in the future will simultaneously lock in the price of product by purchasing futures contracts. By this process, product may be obtained more cheaply and without paying storage costs. If futures prices are selling at a premium to cash there will be an incentive to store the commodity and hedge inventories in futures markets. Futures markets in this case will pay part or all of the storage costs. Thus, futures markets provide signals which help serve the function of allocating product over time and tend to smooth out seasonal variations of supply and demand in the cash market.

The ability to hedge price risk in futures markets smoothes the flow of commerce and facilitates planning by market participants. Because firms can lock in the buying and selling prices of petroleum products ahead of time, the market is less subject to shocks and shortages. This lowers the risk of doing business for market participants. As a result of this, lower profit margins are acceptable and these benefits may be passed on to the consuming public in the form of lower energy prices and a lowered possibility of energy shortages.

The futures market has enhanced the over-the-counter (OTC) market by allowing companies the ability to offer various new instruments of risk management. Derivatives, forwards, swaps, and specialized types of options are some of the products on the OTC market. However, it is the futures market that permits the companies selling OTC products to hedge their own price exposure.

Futures and options markets also provide a mechanism whereby the investing public can benefit from changes in energy prices. Futures contracts are denominated in small enough units that it is economical for small traders to use them. Before there were energy futures markets the only vehicle available to the public was to invest in the stock of energy-related firms.

# STRUCTURAL CHANGES IN THE ENERGY INDUSTRY

During the 1970s, price controls imposed by the federal government in response to the energy shortages caused by OPEC gave favorable price breaks to small refiners. This two-tiered pricing system for oil and gas supported many small refineries which otherwise would not have been able to survive in the marketplace. In addition, this two-tiered pricing system cost the consuming public many millions of dollars in extra energy costs.

The decontrol of oil prices has resulted in a trend toward consolidation in the oil industry. Small refineries, no longer protected by price controls, are unable to compete and are being absorbed by larger, more efficient firms. Even larger oil companies are slowly buying out or merging with similarly sized competitors. These changes are occurring worldwide as even foreign producers are purchasing downstream capacity which gives them the ability to market refined products worldwide. Most notable in this trend are the Saudi Arabians, the Venezuelans, and the Mexicans who are achieving increasing penetration into final product markets and increased sophistication in downstream operations by either purchasing refineries or negotiating deals to supply a crude oil stream to a refiner.

Another important trend involves the demise of the posted pricing system. The oil industry once depended on the rigid pricing system of posted prices where approximately 75% of all crude oil traded at posted prices and only about 25% traded in the spot market. In general it was only the marginal barrels that traded in the spot market. Increasingly, crude oil is trading at spot market prices and posted prices are changing on a regular basis to reflect spot prices. In essence, it is the market, rather than OPEC and the major oil companies, that is driving oil prices.

As the posted pricing system disappears, oil prices change much more often and much more rapidly in response to supply and demand. Futures and options markets are playing an important role in determining spot market prices since the futures market serves as a highly visible, widely, and instantaneously available proxy for spot market prices. Thus, futures markets are providing a price discovery mechanism for energy markets.

As a result of decontrol of natural gas prices in the 1980s, and of electricity in the 1990s, similar consolidations and economies of scale are affecting gas and electric companies. Greater visibility of natural gas and electricity prices in the futures market has spurred the development of the spot market.

The highly visible price discovery mechanism is contributing to a reduction of the number of energy trading firms. Prior to the advent of energy futures markets, energy-trading companies provided middleman services by keeping track of the posted energy prices in different markets and stood ready to buy and sell at advantageous prices. Users of product, lacking the expertise to search out the lowest prices, obtained product from trading firms and in the process paid a higher price than otherwise would have occurred. These higher prices were passed along to the public. With the advent of futures prices, everyone knows the prices of crude oil, heating oil, gasoline, natural gas, propane, and electricity. Thus, there are far fewer opportunities for energy-trading firms to earn profits, sometimes forcing them out of business, and, finally, resulting in lower prices which are passed along to the consuming public.

Prior to the development of energy futures markets, small jobbers and small oil companies were dependent on major suppliers for product and had to rely on the posted price to determine the price. Currently, these smaller firms are in a better negotiating position vis-a-vis their suppliers, because they are in a position to know the current market prices of product.

## FINANCIAL INNOVATIONS

Companies with proven reserves in the ground are often hampered by an inability to finance further exploration by borrowing against their reserves. Banks will lend money only against a small percentage of reserves because of the inability to determine the value of these reserves in advance.

It is currently possible to trade futures contracts for delivery of crude oil as far as seven years in the future. This means that companies may hedge the prices of crude oil in the ground. Because of this ability, banks are willing to lend against a much higher percentage of proven reserves. In order to hedge, the company merely sells futures contracts against its inventory. If oil prices fall, then the futures contracts will generate a profit which protects the value of the bank's collateral.

Another financial innovation involving energy futures markets is called an EFP, or Exchange of Futures for Physicals. Suppose that a buyer and a seller want to conduct a deal involving delivery of product in six months, but they cannot agree upon a price. The seller may want to fix the transaction at the current price, but the buyer may feel that prices will fall in the future. The solution to this problem is to do an exchange of futures for physicals. This is accomplished as follows—the two parties agree that the transaction will take place at the settlement price of a particular futures contract on a particular date in about six months. The seller will short futures contracts when he feels that the price is at its highest and the buyer will purchase futures contracts when he feels that the price is at its lowest. Neither party knows the other's contract prices. On the agreed-upon date the product will change hands at the settlement price of the futures contract and the participants will also enter into a prearranged EFP transaction at the same price to liquidate each other's futures positions. This EFP will take place on the exchange. Transactions done at locations remote from the delivery point of the futures contracts may involve premiums or discounts from the futures price. It is not necessary for delivery to take place on the same date that the EFP occurs on the exchange.

The net effect of an EFP is that both parties are able to lock in the price they judge to be the most advantageous. Through the use of EFPs, the futures market serves as a conduit whereby buyers and sellers are able to arrange product transactions and simultaneously arrange mutually advantageous financial conditions. EFPs have been widely accepted by both buyers and sellers as an important trading tool.

Another use of futures markets, which is apparently very widespread but little known, is the practice of what is called "counter" trading. Often foreign oil producers want to conduct a swap of oil for goods without converting the oil into U.S. dollars to pay for the goods. Once the deal is arranged and the contract signed, the companies which are supplying goods to the foreign producers hedge the price of oil they are to receive in the future by shorting crude oil futures contracts. In effect they lock in the price they will receive for the oil which is to be delivered to them in the future.

The ability of energy suppliers to hedge prices, and thereby offer long-term, firm price contracts to end-users, provides a very valuable service. This "bid business" concept is finding increasing use as suppliers learn how to use futures markets to offer fixed prices to their customers as far as a year or more in the future.

Long-term, firm price contracts offer numerous advantages to end-users. For instance, consider the municipality that is able to contract long term for its heating oil, natural gas, or gasoline needs. The firm price contract means that it is able to budget effectively without the worry of possibly having to increase taxes or transportation fares to pay for increased energy costs.

Many oil refineries are using the heating oil and gasoline futures markets to lock in refinery margins. During those time periods when heating oil and gasoline futures offer the opportunity to lock in a favorable margin over the cost of crude oil, refineries will sell futures contracts in a manner analogous to the crack spreads discussed in chapter 4. Refineries will lock in margins as far into the future as is both feasible and profitable.

The use of options, another financial innovation, offers enormous benefits to energy firms which may, for example, buy calls to guarantee a customer a maximum price over a specific time, or write covered calls to protect inventory. The possibilities for different types of trades using options are endless, especially in conjunction with the use of futures contracts. Although options trading volumes have increased over the years, the use of options has gained only limited acceptance in the energy industry, which believes that trading options is much more complicated than trading futures.

# Structural Changes in the Futures Industry

Over the past several years the futures industry, like the energy industry, has been consolidating. NYMEX bought the Commodity Exchange, Inc. (COMEX), and the New York Cotton Exchange and the Coffee, Sugar and Cocoa Exchange merged into the New York Board of Trade. In addition, while NYMEX had over 80 clearing member firms in the early 1980s, that number has now dwindled to only 49. Wall Street firms have merged assets, offices, and brokers to secure a stronger foothold in the global economy. Consolidation has reduced choices for consumers but has also reduced trading costs.

With the advancement of the use of computers and global telecommunications, the 24-hour trading day has become a reality. Not everyone likes the expanded trading period, but few oppose it for fear of being left behind. The NYMEX ACCESS[SM] system expands the trading day to almost 24 hours, thereby allowing the energy industry to hedge at any hour of day or night instead of waiting until the market opens on the next business day which could expose the company to unforeseen risks.

Commodity exchanges are not only competing with other commodity exchanges but also with their member firms. Some member firms are offering their clients such additional financial tools as exchanges, swaps, and derivatives, instruments that are guaranteed only by the assets of the company selling them.

In conclusion, changes in both the energy and futures industries have resulted in innovative uses of energy futures and options by energy suppliers and consumers. Energy futures and options offer tremendous opportunities for energy firms to increase profits and reduce risk in the future. Having achieved broad appeal and usefulness in the energy industry, there is every indication that the success and importance of energy futures and options will continue to grow. As the number of contracts on different energy products proliferates and volume and open interest grow, risk reduction techniques using futures and options contracts will be increasingly integrated into the everyday operations of the energy industry. The benefits of futures and options trading will continue to accrue to both the energy industry and the consuming public.

# Appendices

The Appendices contain the contract specifications for 13 energy futures/options contracts in an abridged format. Should greater detail be required, please contact the applicable exchange.

# APPENDIX A

## New York Mercantile Exchange No. 2 Heating Oil Futures and Options Contract Specifications

### Trading unit
Futures: 42,000 U.S. gallons (1,000 barrels).
Options: One heating oil futures contract.

### Trading hours
Futures and options: 9:50 A.M. to 3:10 P.M. for open outcry session.
After-hours trading is conducted via the NYMEX ACCESS℠ electronic trading system from 4:00 P.M. Monday through Thursday to 9:00 A.M. the following day and from 7:00 P.M. Sunday to 9:00 A.M. the following day. All times are New York time.

### Trading months
Futures: Trading is conducted in 18 consecutive months commencing with the next calendar month.
Options: 12 consecutive months.

### Price quotation
Futures and options: In dollars and cents per gallon.

### Minimum price fluctuation
Futures and options: $.0001 (.01 cent) per gallon ($4.20 per contract).

### Maximum daily price fluctuation
Futures: Initial maximum price fluctuation is $.20 per gallon for the first two contract months and $.04 per gallon for the back months. In the event of a $.20 per gallon move in either of the first two contract months, trading is halted for one hour; the market is reopened with an additional $.20 per gallon limit for the first two contract months, and back month limits are expanded to $.20 per gallon from the limit then in place. In the event of a $.04 per gallon move in the back months, the back month limit rises on the next trading day to $.06 per gallon. There are no price limits during the last 30 minutes on the last day of trading in the spot month.
Options: No price limits.

## Last trading day
Futures: Trading terminates at the close of business on the last business day of the month preceding the delivery month.
Options: Trading terminates three business days before the underlying futures contract.

## Exercise of options
By a clearing member to the exchange clearinghouse not later than 5:30 P.M., or 45 minutes after the underlying futures settlement price is posted, whichever is later, on any day up to and including the option's expiration.

## Options strike prices
Ten strike prices in $.02 increments above the at-the-money strike price and 10 strike prices in $.02 increments below the at-the-money strike price for a total of at least 21 strike prices. In addition, $.01 strike prices are listed for the first three months listed at $.04 above and below the at-the-money strike price. One cent ($.01) strike prices will only be listed at levels below $1.00.

## Delivery
F.O.B. seller's facility in New York Harbor, ex-shore. All duties, entitlements, taxes, fees, and other charges paid. Requirements for seller's shore facility: capability to deliver into barges. Buyer may request delivery by truck, if available at the seller's facility, and pay a surcharge for truck delivery. Delivery may also be completed by pipeline, tanker, book transfer, or inter- or intra-facility transfer. Delivery must be made in accordance with applicable federal, state, and local licensing and tax laws.

## Delivery period
Deliveries may only be initiated the day after the fifth business day and must be completed before the last business day of the delivery month.

## Alternate delivery procedure (ADP)
An ADP is available to buyers and sellers who have been matched by the exchange subsequent to the termination of trading in the spot month contract. If buyer and seller agree to consummate delivery under terms different from those prescribed in the contract specifications, they may proceed on that basis after submitting a notice of their intention to the exchange.

### Exchange of futures for, or in connection with, physicals (EFP)

The buyer or seller may exchange a futures position for a physical position of equal quantity by submitting a notice to the exchange. EFPs may be used to either initiate or liquidate a futures position.

### Grade and quality specifications

The oil shall be a hydrocarbon oil free from alkali, mineral acid, grit, fibrous or other foreign matter, meeting the specifications set below:

| | |
|---|---|
| Gravity: | API 30°F minimum |
| Flash: | 130°F minimum |
| Viscosity: | Kinematic, Centistokes at 100°F, minimum 2.0, maximum 3.6 |
| Water and sediment: | 0.05% maximum |
| Pour point: | 0°F maximum for contract months September through March; 10°F maximum for contract months April through August |
| Distillation: | 10% point, 480°F maximum; 90% point, 640°F maximum; end point 690°F maximum |
| Sulfur: | 0.20% maximum |
| Thermal stability: | 90 minutes 300°F Pad rating 7 maximum |
| Oxidation stability: | mg/100 ml, maximum 2.5 |
| Haze rating: | 25°C (77°F), Procedure 2, 2 maximum |
| Carbon residue: | Weight % on 10% bottom, 0.35% maximum |
| Ash: | 0.01 wt. % maximum |
| Corrosion: | 3 hours 50°C (122°F), 1 maximum |
| Cloud point: | 15°F maximum for contract months September through March; 20°F maximum for contract months April through August |
| Dye: | All heating oil delivered against this contract, regardless of sulfur content, shall be dyed in satisfaction of the dyeing requirements as prescribed by the Internal Revenue Service (IRS) for tax-free sales or uses of diesel fuel (using the PetroSpec dye analyzer or the IRS Test Method), pursuant to Section 4082 of the Internal Revenue Code of 1986, as Amended. |

### Inspection

The buyer may request an inspection for grade and quality or quantity for all deliveries, but shall require a quantity inspection for a barge, tanker, or inter-facility transfer. If the buyer does not request a quantity inspection, the seller may request such inspection. The cost of the quantity inspection is shared equally by the buyer and seller. If the product meets grade and quality specifications, the cost of the quality inspection is shared jointly by the buyer and seller. If the product fails inspection, the cost is borne by the seller.

# APPENDIX B

## New York Mercantile Exchange
## New York Harbor Unleaded Gasoline Futures
## and Options Contract Specifications

### Trading unit
Futures: 42,000 U.S. gallons (1,000 barrels).
Options: One New York Harbor unleaded gasoline futures contract.

### Trading hours
Futures and options: 9:50 A.M. to 3:10 P.M. for open outcry session.
After-hours trading is conducted via the NYMEX ACCESS℠ electronic trading system from 4:00 P.M. Monday through Thursday to 9:00 A.M. the following day and from 7:00 P.M. Sunday to 9:00 A.M. the following day. All times are New York time.

### Trading months
Futures: Trading is conducted in 18 consecutive months commencing with the next calendar month.
Options: 12 consecutive months.

### Price quotation
Futures and options: In dollars and cents per gallon.

### Minimum price fluctuation
Futures and options: $.0001 (.01 cent) per gallon ($4.20 per contract).

### Maximum daily price fluctuation
Futures: Initial maximum price fluctuation is $.20 per gallon for the first two contract months and $.04 per gallon for the back months. In the event of a $.20 per gallon move in either of the first two contract months, trading is halted for one hour; the market is reopened with an additional $.20 per gallon limit for the first two contract months, and back month limits are expanded to $.20 per gallon from the limit then in place. In the event of a $.04 per gallon move in the back months, the back month limit rises on the next trading day to $.06 per gallon. There are no price limits during the last thirty minutes on the last day of trading in the spot month.
Options: No price limits.

### Last trading day
Futures: Trading terminates at the close of business on the last business day of the month preceding the delivery month.
Options: Trading terminates three business days before the underlying futures contract.

### Exercise of options
By a clearing member to the exchange clearinghouse not later than 5:30 P.M., or 45 minutes after the underlying futures settlement price is posted, whichever is later, on any day up to and including the option's expiration.

### Options strike prices
Twenty strike prices in $.01 increments above and below the at-the-money strike price and 10 strike prices in $.05 increments above the highest and below the lowest existing strike prices for a total of 61 strike prices. The at-the-money strike price is the nearest to the previous day's close of the underlying futures contract. Strike price boundaries are adjusted according to the futures price movements.

### Delivery
F.O.B. seller's facility in New York Harbor, ex-shore. All duties, entitlements, taxes, fees, and other charges paid. Seller's shore facility must meet minimum requirements for water depth and must have the capability to deliver into barges. Delivery may also be completed by pipeline, tanker, book transfer, or inter- or intra-facility transfer. Delivery must be made in accordance with applicable federal, state, and local licensing and tax laws.

### Delivery period
Deliveries may only be initiated the day after the fifth business day and must be completed before the last business day of the delivery month.

### Alternate delivery procedure (ADP)

An ADP is available to buyers and sellers who have been matched by the exchange subsequent to the termination of trading in the spot month contract. If buyer and seller agree to consummate delivery under terms different from those prescribed in the contract specifications, they may proceed on that basis after submitting a notice of their intention to the exchange.

### Exchange of futures for, or in connection with, physicals (EFP)

The buyer or seller may exchange a futures position for a physical position of equal quantity by submitting a notice to the exchange. EFPs may be used to either initiate or liquidate a futures position.

### Grade and quality specifications

The gasoline shall be a hydrocarbon oil free from alkali, mineral acid, grit, fibrous or other foreign matter, meeting the specifications of the Colonial Pipeline Company (Atlanta, Georgia) in effect at the time of delivery, for fungible A grade 87 Octane Index Gasoline or any other fungible grade 87 Octane Index Gasoline listed by the Colonial Pipeline as being properly designated for sale as Reformulated Gasoline in accordance with EPA regulations, provided, however, and notwithstanding anything to the contrary in the Colonial Pipeline specifications, the specifications set below are met:

| | |
|---|---|
| Gravity: | API 52° minimum |
| Lead: | Maximum 0.03 grams per gallon |
| Octane: | (RON+MON)/2 maximum less than 91.0. |
| Oxygen: | 1.7% min by weight |
| Benzene: | 1.3% max by volume |
| Volatile organic compounds emissions: | Min reduction of 23.4% from 1990 baseline for VOC emissions |
| Reid vapor pressure can be no greater than the following maximum levels: | January and February: 15.0 psi<br>March: 13.5 psi<br>April 1 to September 15: n/a<br>September 16 to October 31: 13.5 psi<br>November and December: 15.0 psi |

### Inspection

The buyer may request an inspection for grade and quality or quantity for all deliveries, but shall require a quantity inspection for a barge, tanker, or inter-facility transfer. If the buyer does not request a quantity inspection, the seller may request such inspection. The cost of the quantity inspection is shared equally by the buyer and seller. If the product meets grade and quality specifications, the cost of the quality inspection is shared jointly by the buyer and seller. If the product fails inspection, the cost is borne by the seller.

# APPENDIX C

## New York Mercantile Exchange Light, Sweet Crude Oil Futures and Options Contract Specifications

### Trading unit
Futures: 1,000 U.S. barrels (42,000 gallons).
Options: One light, sweet crude oil futures contract.

### Trading hours
Futures and options: 9:45 A.M. to 3:10 P.M. for open outcry session.
After-hours trading is conducted via the NYMEX ACCESS℠ electronic trading system from 4:00 P.M. Monday through Thursday to 9:00 A.M. the following day and from 7:00 P.M. Sunday to 9:00 A.M. the following day. All times are New York time.

### Trading months
Futures: Trading is conducted in 30 consecutive months commencing with the next calendar month plus long-dated contracts initially listed at 48, 60, 72, and 84 months prior to delivery. Additionally, trading can be executed at an average differential to the previous day's settlement prices for periods of 2 to 30 consecutive months in a single transaction. These calendar strips are executed during open outcry trading hours.
Options: 12 consecutive months plus 3 long-dated options initially listed at 18, 24, and 36 months out on a June–December cycle.

### Price quotation
Futures and options: In dollars and cents per barrel.

### Minimum price fluctuation
Futures and options: $.01 per barrel ($10 per contract).

### Maximum daily price fluctuation
Futures: Initial maximum price fluctuation is $7.50 per barrel for the first two contract months and $1.50 per barrel for the back months. In the event of a $7.50 per barrel move in either of the first two contract months, trading is halted for one

hour; the market is reopened with an additional $7.50 per barrel limit for the first two contract months, and back month limits are expanded to $7.50 per barrel from the limit then in place. In the event of a $1.50 per barrel move in the back months, the back month limit rises on the next trading day to $3.00 per barrel. There are no price limits during the last 30 minutes on the last day of trading in the spot month.
Options: No price limits.

### Last trading day
Futures: Trading terminates at the close of business on the third business day prior to the 25th calendar day of the month preceding the delivery month.
Options: Trading terminates three business days before the underlying futures contract.

### Exercise of options
By a clearing member to the exchange clearinghouse not later than 5:30 P.M., or 45 minutes after the underlying futures settlement price is posted, whichever is later, on any day up to and including the option's expiration.

### Options strike prices
Twenty strike prices in increments of $.50 per barrel above and below the at-the-money strike price and the next 10 strike prices in increments of $2.50 above the highest and below the lowest existing strike prices for a total of 61 strike prices. The at-the-money strike price is the nearest to the previous day's close of the underlying futures contract. Strike price boundaries are adjusted according to the futures price movements.

### Delivery
F.O.B. seller's facility, Cushing, Oklahoma, at any pipeline or storage facility with pipeline access to TEPPCO, Cushing Storage, or Equilon Pipeline Co., by in-tank transfer, in-line transfer, book-out or inter-facility transfer (pumpover).

### Delivery period
All deliveries are ratable over the course of the month and must be initiated on or after the first calendar day and completed by the last calendar day of the delivery month.

### Alternate delivery procedure (ADP)

An ADP is available to buyers and sellers who have been matched by the exchange subsequent to the termination of trading in the spot month contract. If buyer and seller agree to consummate delivery under terms different from those prescribed in the contract specifications, they may proceed on that basis after submitting a notice of their intention to the exchange.

### Exchange of futures for, or in connection with, physicals (EFP)

The commercial buyer or seller may exchange a futures position for a physical position of equal quantity by submitting a notice to the exchange. EFPs may be used to either initiate or liquidate a futures position.

### Deliverable grades

Specific domestic crudes with 0.42% sulfur by weight or less, not less than 37° API gravity nor more than 42° API gravity. The following domestic crude streams are deliverable: West Texas Intermediate, Low Sweet Mix, New Mexican Sweet, North Texas Sweet, Oklahoma Sweet, and South Texas Sweet.

Specific foreign crudes of not less than 34° API nor more than 42° API. The following foreign streams are deliverable: U.K. Brent and Forties, and Norwegian Oseberg Blend, for which the seller shall receive a $.30 per barrel discount below the final settlement price; Nigerian Bonny Light and Colombian Cusiana, delivered at a $.15 premium; and Nigerian Qua Iboe, delivered at a $.05 premium.

### Inspection

Inspection shall be conducted in accordance with pipeline practices. A buyer or seller may appoint an inspector to inspect the quality of oil delivered. However, the buyer or seller who requests the inspection will bear its costs and will notify the party of the transaction that the inspection will occur.

# APPENDIX D

# New York Mercantile Exchange Henry Hub Natural Gas Futures and Options Contract Specifications

### Trading unit
Futures: 10,000 Million British thermal units (MMBtu).
Options: One Henry Hub natural gas futures contract.

### Trading hours
Futures and options: 9:30 A.M. to 3:10 P.M. for open outcry session.
After-hours trading is conducted via the NYMEX ACCESS℠ electronic trading system from 4:00 P.M. Monday through Thursday to 9:00 A.M. the following day and from 7:00 P.M. Sunday to 9:00 A.M. the following day. All times are New York time.

### Trading months
Futures: Trading is conducted in 36 consecutive months commencing with the next calendar month.
Options: 12 consecutive months plus long-dated options initially listed at 15, 18, 21, 24, 27, 30, 33,and 36 months out on a June–December cycle.

### Price quotation
Futures and options: In dollars and cents per MMBtu.

### Minimum price fluctuation
Futures and options: $.001 (.1 cent) per MMBtu ($10 per contract).

## Maximum daily price fluctuation

Futures: Initial maximum price fluctuation is $.75 per MMBtu for the first two contract months and $.15 per MMBtu for the back months. In the event of a $.75 per MMBtu move in either of the first two contract months, trading is halted for one hour; the market is reopened with an additional $.75 per MMBtu limit for the first two contract months, and back month limits are expanded to $.75 per MMBtu from the limit then in place. In the event of a $.15 per MMBtu move in the back months, the back month limit rises on the next trading day to $.30 per MMBtu. There are no price limits during the last thirty minutes on the last day of trading in the spot month.

Options: No price limits.

## Last trading day

Futures: Trading terminates three business days prior to the first day of the delivery month.

Options: Trading terminates at the close of business on the business day immediately preceding the expiration of the underlying futures contract.

## Exercise of options

By a clearing member to the exchange clearinghouse not later than 5:30 P.M., or 45 minutes after the underlying futures settlement price is posted, whichever is later, on any day up to and including the option's expiration.

## Options strike prices

Twenty strike prices in increments of $.05 per MMBtu above and below the at-the-money strike price and the next 10 strike prices in increments of $.25 above the highest and below the lowest existing strike prices for a total of 61 strike prices. The at-the-money strike price is the nearest to the previous day's close of the underlying futures contract. Strike price boundaries are adjusted according to the futures price movements.

## Delivery location

Sabine Pipe Line Co.'s Henry Hub in Louisiana. Seller is responsible for the movement of the gas through the Hub; the buyer, from the Hub. The Hub fee will be paid by the seller.

### Delivery period

Delivery shall take place no earlier than the first calendar day of the delivery month and completed no later than the last calendar day of the delivery month. All deliveries shall be made at as uniform as possible an hourly and daily rate of flow over the course of the delivery month, unless amended by mutual agreement of the participants.

### Alternate delivery procedure (ADP)

An ADP is available to buyers and sellers who have been matched by the exchange subsequent to the termination of trading in the spot month contract. If buyer and seller agree to consummate delivery under terms different from those prescribed in the contract specifications, they may proceed on that basis after submitting a notice of their intention to the exchange.

### Exchange of futures for, or in connection with, physicals (EFP)

The commercial buyer or seller may exchange a futures position for a physical position of equal quantity by submitting a notice to the exchange. EFPs may be used to either initiate or liquidate a futures position.

# APPENDIX E

## New York Mercantile Exchange Propane Futures Contract Specifications

**Trading unit**
42,000 U.S. gallons (1,000 barrels).

**Trading hours**
8:30 A.M. to 2:40 P.M. for open outcry session.
After-hours trading is conducted via the NYMEX ACCESS℠ electronic trading system from 5:00 P.M. to 7:00 P.M. Monday through Thursday. All times are New York time.

**Trading months**
Trading is conducted in 15 consecutive months commencing with the next calendar month.

**Price quotation**
In dollars and cents per gallon.

**Minimum price fluctuation**
$.0001 (.01 cent) per gallon ($4.20 per contract).

**Maximum daily price fluctuation**
Initial maximum price fluctuation is $.20 per gallon for the first two contract months and $.04 per gallon for the back months. In the event of a $.20 per gallon move in either of the first two contract months, trading is halted for one hour; the market is reopened with an additional $.20 per gallon limit for the first two contract months, and back month limits are expanded to $.20 per gallon from the limit then in place. In the event of a $.04 per gallon move in the back months, the back month limit rises on the next trading day to $.06 per gallon. There are no price limits during the last thirty minutes on the last day of trading in the spot month.

### Last trading day
Trading terminates at the close of business on the last business day of the month preceding the delivery month.

### Delivery
F.O.B. at Texas Eastern Products Pipeline Co. or, with the agreement of the buyer and the seller, at any pipeline, storage facility or fractionation facility in Mont Belvieu, Texas, with direct pipeline access to TEPPCO. Delivery may be made by in-line or in-well transfer, inter-facility transfer from the seller's facility to TEPPCO, or by book transfer, unless either the buyer or the seller disagrees with such transfer.

### Delivery period
Deliveries must be initiated after the fourth business day and completed by the calendar day prior to the last business day of the delivery month.

### Alternate delivery procedure (ADP)
An ADP is available to buyers and sellers who have been matched by the exchange subsequent to the termination of trading in the spot month contract. If buyer and seller agree to consummate delivery under terms different from those prescribed in the contract specifications, they may proceed on that basis after submitting a notice of their intention to the exchange.

### Exchange of futures for, or in connection with, physicals (EFP)
The buyer or seller may exchange a futures position for a physical position of equal quantity by submitting a notice to the exchange. EFPs may be used to either initiate or liquidate a futures position.

### Grade and quality specifications
Conforms to industry standards for fungible liquefied propane gas as determined by the Gas Processors Association (GPA-HD5).

### Inspection
Inspection shall be conducted in accordance with pipeline practices.

# APPENDIX F

# New York Mercantile Exchange Four Electricity (Palo Verde, California–Oregon Border, Cinergy, Entergy) Futures and Options Contract Specifications

### Trading unit
Futures: Palo Verde and California–Oregon Border: 432 megawatt hours; Cinergy and Entergy: 736 megawatt hours, all delivered over a monthly period. Options: One electricity futures contract.

### Trading hours
Futures and options: Trading is conducted via the NYMEX ACCESS℠ electronic trading system from 4:00 P.M. to 2:30 P.M. the next day Monday through Thursday, and from 7:00 P.M. Sunday to 2:30 P.M. Monday. All times are New York time.

### Trading months
Futures: Trading is conducted in 18 consecutive months commencing with the next calendar month.
Options: 12 consecutive months.

### Price quotation
Futures and options: In dollars and cents per Mwh.

### Minimum price fluctuation
Futures and options: $.01 per Mwh ($4.32 or $7.36 per contract).

### Maximum daily price fluctuation
Futures: Palo Verde and California–Oregon Border: Initial maximum price fluctuation is $7.50 per Mwh for the first two contract months and $3.00 per Mwh for the back months. In the event of a $7.50 per Mwh move in either of the first

two contract months, trading is halted for one hour; the market is reopened with an additional $7.50 per Mwh limit for the first two contract months, and back month limits are expanded to $7.50 per Mwh from the limit then in place. In the event of a $3.00 per Mwh move in the back months, the back month limit rises on the next trading day to $6.00 per Mwh. There are no price limits during the last 30 minutes on the last day of trading in the spot month.

Cinergy and Entergy: Initial maximum price fluctuation is $10.00 per Mwh. There are no price limits during the last one hour of trading on the last two trading days in the spot month. Contact NYMEX for special price fluctuation limits.

Options: No price limits.

### Last trading day

Futures: Trading terminates on the fourth business day prior to the first day of the delivery month.

Options: Trading terminates on the day preceding the expiration of the underlying futures contract.

### Exercise of options

By a clearing member to the exchange clearinghouse not later than 5:30 P.M., or 45 minutes after the underlying futures settlement price is posted, whichever is later, on any day up to and including the option's expiration.

### Options strike prices

Five strike prices in $1.00 per Mwh increments above the at-the-money strike price and five strike prices in $1.00 per Mwh increments below the at-the-money strike price.

### Delivery rate

Two Mw throughout every hour of the delivery period (this can be amended upon mutual agreement of the buyer and seller).

### Delivery period

Sixteen on-peak hours: hour ending 0700 prevailing time to hour ending 2200 prevailing time (6:00 A.M. to 10:00 P.M.). This can also be amended at the time of delivery by mutual consent of the buyer and seller.

### Scheduling

Buyer and seller must follow Western Systems Coordinating Council scheduling practices.

### Alternate delivery procedure (ADP)

An ADP is available to buyers and sellers who have been matched by the exchange subsequent to the termination of trading in the spot month contract. If buyer and seller agree to consummate delivery under terms different from those prescribed in the contract specifications, they may proceed on that basis after submitting a notice of their intention to the exchange.

### Exchange of futures for, or in connection with, physicals (EFP)

The commercial buyer or seller may exchange a futures position for a physical position of equal quantity by submitting a notice to the exchange. EFPs may be used to either initiate or liquidate a futures position.

# APPENDIX G

# International Petroleum Exchange Gas Oil Futures and Options Contract Specifications

### Trading unit
Futures: 100 metric tons.
Options: One gas oil futures contract.

### Trading hours
Futures: 8:00 A.M. to 9:00 A.M. (electronic);
  9:15 A.M. to 5:27 P.M. (open outcry) London time.
Options: 9:15 A.M. to 5:25 P.M. London time.

### Trading months
Futures: Trading is conducted in 12 consecutive months, then quarterly out to a maximum of 18 months.
Options: The first six quoted months of the gas oil futures contract, with a new position being introduced immediately on expiration of the first option month.

### Price quotation
Futures and options: In U.S. dollars and cents per ton (on an EU import duty paid basis).

### Minimum price fluctuation
Futures: U.S. $.25 per ton ($25.00 per contract).
Options: U.S. $.05 per ton ($5.00 per contract).

### Maximum daily price fluctuation
Futures and options: No price limits.

### Last trading day
Futures: Trading terminates at 12:00 P.M. (noon) two business days prior to the 14th calendar day of the delivery month. This date is also the tender day.
Options: Trading terminates at the close of business on the fifth business day prior to termination of trading in the underlying gas oil futures contract.

### Exercise and automatic exercise of options

Gas oil options can be exercised into gas oil futures contracts. IPE options contracts are of American-style exercise, allowing the buyer to exercise call and/or put options up to 5:00 P.M. on any business day (except on the expiration day) during the life of the contracts, by giving an exercise notice to the London Clearing House.

On the day of expiration the buyer has up to one hour after the termination of trading to exercise his options, after which time the London Clearing House will automatically exercise all options that are in the money unless instructed otherwise.

### Options strike prices

Multiples of U.S. $5.00 per ton.

A minimum of five strike prices for each contract month: one nearest to the previous business day's settlement price for that month; two (or more) above and two (or more) below that price. During any trading day the exchange may add one or more strike prices nearest to the last price listed.

### Delivery and delivery period

Delivery of one or more lots of 100 metric tons of gas oil, with delivery by volume (namely, 118.35 cubic meters per lot being the equivalent of 100 tons of gas oil at a density of 0.845 kg/liter in vacuum at 15°C), may be made into barge or coaster or by in-tank or inter-tank transfer from Customs and Excise bonded storage installations or refineries in the Amsterdam, Rotterdam, Antwerp (A.R.A.) area (including Vissingen and Ghent) between the sixteenth and the last calendar day of the delivery month.

Gas oil shall be delivered in bulk and free of all liens and claims and be of merchantable quality conforming to the quality specified by the IPE.

### Alternate delivery procedure (ADP)

The contract provides for matched buyers and sellers, by agreement, to deliver gas oil of a different specification or in a manner, or in a location, or on terms other than those specified. In the event of an ADP, the London Clearing House ceases to have any obligation to the buyer or the seller.

### Exchange for physicals (EFP) and exchange for swaps (EFS)

EFPs and EFSs may take place at any time up to one hour after termination of trading in the delivery month in which the EFP or the EFS is traded.

## Grade and quality specifications

| | |
|---|---|
| Density: | kg/liter at 15°C, 0.820 minimum; 0.860 maximum |
| Distillation: | Evaporated at 250°C, 65% volume maximum; evaporated at 350°C, 85% volume minimum |
| Color: | 2.0 maximum |
| Flash point: | Pensky Martens "Closed Cup": 55°C minimum |
| Total sulfur: | 0.20% weight maximum |
| Viscosity: | Kinematic, Centistokes at 20°C, maximum 6.0 |
| Cloud point: | 1°C maximum for contract months October through March; 5°C maximum for contract months April through September |
| Cold filter plugging point: | −11°C maximum for contract months October through March; −4°C maximum for contract months April through September |
| Oxygen stability | mg/100 ml, maximum 3.0 |
| Cetane index: | 45 minimum |
| Sediment: | mg/kg, 30 maximum |
| Water: | mg/kg, 200 maximum |
| Strong acid number: | mg KoH/gm, 0.1 maximum |
| Halogenated hydrocarbons: | Not detected |

## Law

The contract is governed by English law and includes provisions regarding force majeure, trade emergencies and embargoes.

# APPENDIX H

# International Petroleum Exchange Brent Crude Oil Futures and Options Contract Specifications

### Trading unit
Futures: 1,000 barrels (42,000 U.S. gallons).
Options: One Brent crude oil futures contract.

### Trading hours
Futures:  8:00 A.M. to 9:45 A.M. (electronic);
            10:02 A.M. to 8:13 P.M. (open outcry) London time.
Options: 10:00 A.M. to 8:13 P.M. London time.

### Trading months
Futures: Trading is conducted in 12 consecutive months, then quarterly out to a maximum of 24 months, and then half yearly out to a maximum of 36 months.
Options: The first 6 quoted months of the Brent crude oil futures contract, with a new position being introduced immediately on expiration of the first option month.

### Price quotation
Futures and options: In U.S. dollars and cents per barrel.

### Minimum price fluctuation
Futures and options: U.S. $.01 per barrel ($10 per contract).

### Maximum daily price fluctuation
Futures and options: No price limits.

### Last trading day
Futures: Trading terminates at the close of business on the business day immediately preceding the 15th day prior to the 1st day of the delivery month. If the 15th day is a non-banking day in London (including Saturday), trading terminates on the business day immediately preceding the first business day prior to the 15th day.
Options: Trading terminates at the close of business on the 3rd business day prior to the termination of trading in the underlying futures contract.

## Exercise and automatic exercise of options

Brent crude oil options can be exercised into Brent crude oil futures contracts. IPE options contracts are of American-style exercise, allowing the buyer to exercise call and/or put options up to 5:00 P.M. on any business day (except on the expiration day) during the life of the contracts, by giving an exercise notice to the London Clearing House.

On the day of expiration the buyer has up to one hour after the termination of trading to exercise his options, after which time the London Clearing House will automatically exercise all options that are in the money unless instructed otherwise.

## Options strike prices

Multiples of U.S. $.50 per ton.

A minimum of five strike prices for each contract month: one nearest to the previous business day's settlement price for that month; two (or more) above and two (or more) below that price. During any trading day the exchange may add one or more strike prices nearest to the last price listed.

## Delivery/settlement basis

The futures contract is deliverable based on an Exchange for Physical (EFP) delivery with an option to cash settle against the published settlement price (i.e., the Brent Index price) for the day following the last trading day of the futures contract. Notice must be given to the London Clearing House up to one hour after termination of trading that the contract will be subject to the cash settlement procedure.

The Brent Index, prepared daily by the exchange at 12:00 P.M. (noon) London time, is the weighted average of the prices of all confirmed 15-day Brent deals throughout the previous trading day, for the appropriate delivery month. These prices are published by the independent price reporting services used by the oil industry. The Index is calculated as an average of the following elements:

1. A weighted average of first month trades in the 15-day market
2. A weighted average of second month trades in the 15-day market plus or minus a straight average of the spread trades between the first and second months
3. A straight average of all the assessments published in media reports.

**Exchange for physicals (EFP) and exchange for swaps (EFS)**
EFPs and EFSs may take place at any time up to one hour after termination of trading in the delivery month in which the EFP or the EFS is traded.

**Law**
The contract is governed by English law and includes provisions regarding force majeure, trade emergencies and embargoes.

# APPENDIX I

# International Petroleum Exchange Natural Gas NBP Futures Contract Specifications

### Contract size
I,000 therms per day during the specified delivery period (month or Balance of Month).

### Trading unit
Minimum of five lots of 1,000 therms (5,000 therms) of natural gas each day during the delivery period.

### Trading hours
9:30 A.M. to 5:00 P.M. London time.

### Trading mechanism
Contracts are traded through the IPE automated Energy Trading System (ETS) or by the exchange of futures for physicals (EFPs).

### Trading months
Trading is conducted in a single Balance of Month contract (for any unexpired days remaining in the current month), then in 15 consecutive months beginning with the next whole month.

### Price quotation
In Sterling, in units of pence per therm.

### Minimum price fluctuation
.01 pence per therm (£3.00 per contract).

### Maximum daily price fluctuation
No price limits.

### Last trading day

Trading terminates at the close of business on the business day that is two business days prior to the first calendar day of the delivery month.

Balance of Month contracts terminate at the close of business on the business day that is two business days prior to the penultimate calendar day of the delivery month.

### Contract description

Monthly contracts are traded as groups of individual calendar days; thus, a monthly contract comprises 28, 29, 30 or 31 individual day contracts depending on the number of days in the month in question. Upon delivery, monthly contracts involve delivery, on each day in the delivery month, of the number of lots remaining open upon expiration of the contract.

Balance of Month contracts comprise a string of individual day contracts, but with the precise number determined by the number of days still outstanding in the current month. The Balance of Month contract, therefore, reduces in size on a daily basis generating a daily contract representing the delivery obligation of that day. Seven individual daily contracts are listed from one day ahead to seven days ahead.

Delivery takes place in kilowatt hours using the industry standard conversion factor of 29.3071 kilowatt hours per therm.

### Exchange for physicals (EFP)

EFPs may take place at any time up to 30 minutes after the close of trading and must be registered in accordance with IPE procedures.

### Law

The contract is governed by English law and includes provisions regarding force majeure, trade emergencies and embargoes.

# APPENDIX J

## New York Mercantile Exchange Central Appalachian Coal Futures Contract Specifications

**Trading unit**
1,550 tons.

**Trading hours**
10:30 A.M. to 2:30 P.M. All times are New York time.

**Trading months**
Trading is conducted in 24 to 26 consecutive months commencing with the next calendar month.

**Price quotation**
In dollars and cents per ton.

**Minimum price fluctuation**
$.01 (1 cent) per ton ($15.50 per contract).

**Maximum daily price fluctuation**
$12.00 per ton ($18,600 per contract) for all months. If any contract is traded, bid, or offered at the limit for five minutes, trading is halted for 10 minutes. When trading resumes, expanded limits are in place that allow the price to fluctuate by $24.00 in either direction of the previous day's settlement price. There are no price limits on any month during the last three days of trading in the spot month.

**Last trading day**
Trading terminates on the fourth to the last business day of the month prior to the delivery month.

**Contract Delivery Unit**
The seller shall deliver 1,550 tons of coal per contract. A loading tolerance of 60 tons or 2%, whichever is greater, over the total number of contracts delivered is permitted.

### Delivery Location
Delivery shall be made F.O.B. buyer's barge at seller's delivery facility on the Ohio River between Mileposts 306 and 317, or on the Big Sandy River, with all duties, entitlements, taxes, fees and other charges imposed prior to delivery paid by the seller. There will be a discount of $0.10 per ton below the final settlement price for any delivery to a terminal on the Big Sandy River.

### Heat Content
Minimum of 12,000 Btus per pound, gross calorific value, with an analysis tolerance of 250 Btus per pound below.

### Ash Content
Maximum of 13.50% by weight with no analysis tolerance.

### Sulfur Content
Maximum of 1.00%, with analysis tolerance of 0.050% above.

### Moisture Content
Maximum of 10.00%, with no analysis tolerance.

### Volatile Matter
Minimum of 30.00%, with no analysis tolerance.

### Hardness/Grindability
Minimum 41 Hardgrove Index with three point analysis tolerance below. Hardness measures how difficult it is to pulverize coal for injection into the boiler flame.

### Size
Three inches topsize, nominal, with a maximum of 55% passing one-quarter-inch-square wire cloth sieve or smaller, to be determined on the basis of the primary cutter of the mechanical sampling system.

### Delivery period
Seller shall schedule deliveries from the first calendar day of the delivery month until the 8th to the last calendar day of the delivery month and completed no later than the last calendar day of the delivery month.

### Alternate delivery procedure (ADP)

An ADP is available to buyers and sellers who have been matched by the exchange subsequent to the termination of trading in the spot month contract. If buyer and seller agree to consummate delivery under terms different from those prescribed in the contract specifications, they may proceed on that basis after submitting a notice of their intention to the exchange.

### Exchange of futures for, or in connection with, product (EFP)

The commercial buyer or seller may exchange a futures position for product of equal quantity by submitting a notice to the exchange. EFPs may be used to either initiate or liquidate a futures position. The EFP deadline is 10:00 A.M. (New York time) on the first business day following termination of trading.

# APPENDIX K

## New York Mercantile Exchange Crack Spread Options Contract Specifications

### Type
A 1:1 option on the price differential between either heating oil and crude oil futures, or unleaded gasoline and crude oil futures. Both options series are American options with the same terms and conditions.

### Trading unit
A long crack call, or a short crack put, are defined as the assignment of futures positions involving at exercise one long underlying heating oil or gasoline futures contract and one short crude oil futures contract.

A long crack put, or a short crack call, are defined as the assignment of futures positions involving at exercise one short underlying heating oil or gasoline futures contract and one long crude oil futures contract.

### Trading hours
9:50 A.M. to 3:10 P.M. (consistent with product futures and options).

### Trading months
Trading is conducted in six consecutive months, plus two quarterly months on a March, June September, December rotation.

### Price quotation
Prices are quoted in dollars and cents per barrel.

### Minimum price fluctuation
$.01 (1 cent) per barrel ($10 per contract).

### Maximum daily price fluctuation
There are no price limits.

## Last trading day (expiration day)

Trading terminates the business day before the termination of trading in the underlying crude oil futures contract.

## Exercise of options

Prices for both contracts will be determined by an established algorithm, using the settlement price of crude oil on the day of exercise to price the crude oil leg of the spread. The product leg is priced by taking the crude price, adding the strike price, and rounding to the nearest dollar and cents figure divided by 42. (This will always be within 21 points of the crude price plus the strike price.)

## Options strike prices

An at-the-money strike price is determined by rounding the differential between the product leg and the crude oil leg to the nearest $0.25 interval. Five additional strike prices will be offered both above and below the established at-the-money strike price in $0.25 increments. Also, 3 additional out-of-the-money strike prices will be added above those strike prices determined above. The additional strikes will be calculated by taking the highest/lowest strike from the above series, rounded to the next higher/lower dollar increment. An additional 2 strike prices will be added at $2 intervals above the out-of-the-money strikes.

# Glossary of Commodity Futures and Energy Industry Terms

**Account executive.** The agent of a commission house who serves customers/traders by entering their commodity futures orders, reporting futures trade executions, advising on futures trading strategies, etc.

**Accumulate.** Traders are said to accumulate contracts when they add to their original market position.

**Actuals.** Physical commodities.

**ADP.** Alternative Delivery Procedure. A futures contract provision that allows buyers and sellers to make and take delivery under terms or conditions that differ from those prescribed in the futures contract. An ADP occurs following termination of futures trading in the spot month and after all long and short futures positions have been matched for the purpose of delivery.

**AGA.** American Gas Association.

**Allowances.** The discounts (premiums) allowed for grades or locations of a commodity lower (higher) than the par or a basis grade or location specified in the futures contract; also called differentials.

**American option.** An options contract that may be exercised at any time prior to expiration. This differs from a "European option," which may only be exercised on the expiration date. New York Mercantile Exchange options are "American," except for the five day gold, silver, and copper options that trade on the COMEX Division.

**API.** American Petroleum Institute.

**Arbitrage.** The simultaneous purchase and sale of similar or identical commodities in two different markets in hope of gaining a profit from price differentials.

**Ask.** A motion to sell. The same as offer.

**Assignment.** The process by which the seller of an option is notified of the buyer's intention to exercise the rights associated with the option.

**Associated person (AP).** See *Broker, Customer's Man.*

**ASTM.** American Society for Testing Materials. Grade and quality specifications for petroleum products are determined by ASTM in test methods.

**At the market.** An order placed "at the market" is done immediately at the best price available when it reaches the trading floor.

**At-the-money.** An option whose exercise, or strike, price is closest to the futures price.

**Backwardation.** Market situation in which futures prices are progressively lower in the distant delivery months. For instance, if the crude oil quotation for February is $15 per barrel and that for June is $14 per barrel, the market is in backwardation. (Backwardation is the opposite of contango.) See *Inverted Market.*

**Barrel.** A unit of volume measurement used for petroleum and its products. 1 barrel = 42 U.S. gallons.

**Baseload.** The minimum amount of electric power delivered or required over a period of time at a steady rate.

**Basis.** The differential that exists at any time between the futures price for a given commodity and the comparable cash or spot price for the commodity.

**Basis grade.** The grade of a commodity used as the standard of the contract.

**Basis risk.** The uncertainty as to whether the cash-futures spread will widen or narrow between the time a hedge position is implemented and liquidated.

**Batch.** A measured amount of oil or refined product in a pipeline.

**Bcf.** Billion cubic feet.

**B/D.** Barrels per day. Usually used in connection with a refiner's production capacity or an oilfield's rate of flow.

**Bear.** One who believes the market is headed lower; also, a downtrending market.

**Bear spread.** An options position comprised of long and short options of the same type, either calls or puts, designed to be profitable in a declining market. An option with a lower strike price is sold and one with a higher strike price is bought.

**Bid.** A motion to buy a futures contract at a specified price.

**Black-Scholes model.** An options pricing formula initially derived by Fisher Black and Myron Scholes for securities options and later refined by Mr. Black for options on futures.

**Board of trade.** Any exchange or association, whether incorporated or unincorporated, of persons who are engaged in the business of buying or selling any commodity or receiving the same for sale on consignment (Sec. 2(2) Commodity Exchange Act).

**Board order or market if touched (MIT) order.** An order that becomes a market order when a particular price is reached. A sell MIT is placed above the market; a buy MIT is placed below the market.

**Booking the basis.** A forward pricing sales arrangement in which cash price is determined either by the buyer or seller within a specified time. At that time, the previously agreed basis is applied to the then-current futures quotation.

**Book transfer.** Transfer of title to buyer without physical movement of product.

**Box spread.** An options market arbitrage in which both a bull spread and a bear spread are established for a riskless profit. One spread includes put options and the other includes calls.

**Break.** A rapid and sharp price decline.

**Breakeven point.** The underlying futures price at which a given options strategy is neither profitable nor unprofitable. For call options, it is the strike price plus the premium. For put options, it is the strike price minus the premium.

**British thermal unit (Btu).** The amount of heat required to increase the temperature of one pound of water 1°F.

**Broker.** A person paid a fee or commission for executing buy or sell orders of a customer. In commodity futures trading, the term may refer to (1) *Floor Broker—* a person who actually executes orders on the trading floor of an exchange; (2) *Account Executive, Associated Person, Registered Commodity Representative*, or *Customer's Man*—the person who deals with customers in the offices of futures commission merchants; and (3) the *Futures Commission Merchant*.

**Brokerage.** The fee charged by a broker for execution of a transaction. The fee may be a flat amount or a percentage.

**Bull.** One who believes that prices are headed higher; also, an up-trending market.

**Bull spread.** An options position composed of both long and short options of the same type, either calls or puts, designed to be profitable in a rising market. An option with a lower strike price is bought and one with a higher strike price is sold.

**Bunker fuel oil.** Heavy fuel oil used in ships' boilers.

**Buyer's market.** A condition of the market in which there is an abundance of goods available and hence buyers can afford to be selective and may be able to buy at less than the price that had previously prevailed.

**Buy in.** Making purchase to cover a previous sale; often called covering.

**Buying hedge (or long hedge).** Hedging transaction in which futures contracts are bought to protect against possible increased cost of commodities. See *Hedging*.

**Buy on close.** To buy at the end of the trading session within the closing-price range. (Also may be "sell on close.")

**Buy on opening.** To buy at the beginning of a trading session within the opening-price range. (Also may be "sell on opening.")

**Calendar spread.** An options position comprised of the purchase and sale of two option contracts of the same type that have the same strike prices but different expiration dates. Also known as a horizontal, or time spread.

**Call option.** An option that gives the buyer (holder) the right, but not the obligation, to buy a futures contract (enter into a long futures position) for a specified price within a specified period of time in exchange for a one time premium payment. It obligates the seller (writer) of an option to sell the underlying futures contract (enter into a short futures position) at the designated price, should the option be exercised at that price.

**Carrying charge.** The total cost of storing a commodity; includes actual storage charges, insurance, interest on loans, and opportunity loss on committed capital.

**Cash commodity.** The actual physical commodity. Sometimes called a spot commodity or actuals.

**Cash Market.** The market for a cash commodity where the actual physical product is traded.

**CF/D.** Cubic feet per day. Usually used to quantify the rate of flow of a gas well or pipeline.

**CFTC.** Commodity Futures Trading Commission. The federal regulatory body which oversees commodity futures trading activities, standards, and practices.

**CIF.** Cost, insurance, freight. Term refers to a sale in which the buyer agrees to pay a unit price that includes the FOB value at the port of origin plus all costs of insurance and transportation. This type of transaction differs from a "delivered" agreement in that it is generally ex-duty, and the buyer accepts the quantity and quality at the loading port rather than at the unloading port.

**Class of options.** All call options, or all put options, exercisable for the same underlying futures contract and which expire on the same expiration date.

**Clean cargo.** Refined products: distillate, kerosene, gasoline, and jet fuel carried by tankers, barges, and tank cars; all refined products except bunker fuels and residuals.

**Clearinghouse.** An exchange-associated body charged with the function of insuring the financial integrity of each trade. Orders are "cleared" by means of the clearinghouse becoming the buyer to all sellers and the seller to all buyers.

**Closing range.** A range of prices at which transactions took place at the closing of the market.

**Collar.** A supply contract between a buyer and a seller of a commodity, whereby the buyer is assured that he will not have to pay more than some maximum price and whereby the seller is assured of receiving some minimum price. This is analogous to an options fence, also known as a range forward.

**Commission.** The fee charged by a futures broker for the execution of an order for a futures trade.

**Commission house.** An organization that buys and sells actual commodities and/or futures contracts for the accounts of its customers in return for a fee.

**Commitment or open interest.** The number of futures contracts in existence at any period of time which have not as yet been satisfied by an offsetting sale or purchase or by actual contract delivery.

**Common carrier.** A person or company having state or federal authority to perform public transportation for hire.

**Contango market.** A futures market that is deemed "normal" when carrying charges are reflected in proportionately higher prices for increasingly distant futures contracts.

**Contingency order.** An order which becomes effective upon the fulfillment of some condition in the marketplace.

**Contract grade.** That grade of product established in the rules of a commodity futures exchange as being suitable for delivery against a futures contract.

**Control area.** A large geographic area within which a utility (or group of utilities) regulates electric power generation in order to maintain scheduled interchanges of power with other control areas and to maintain the required system frequency.

**Conversion.** A delta-neutral arbitrage transaction involving a long futures, a long put option, and a short call option. The put and call options have the same strike price and same expiration date.

**Cover.** To close out a short futures position.

**Covered writing.** The sale of an option against an existing position in the underlying futures contract; *e.g.*, short call and long futures.

**Crack spreads.** The simultaneous purchase or sale of crude oil against the sale or purchase of refined petroleum products. These spread differentials, which represent refining margins, are normally quoted in dollars per barrel.

**Cubic feet.** The most common measure of gas volume, referring to the amount of gas needed to fill a volume of one cubic foot at 14.3 pounds per square inch absolute pressure and 60° Fahrenheit. One cubic foot of natural gas contains, on average, 1,027 Btus.

**Day trade.** The purchase and sale of a futures contract on the same day.

**Delivered.** Often regarded as synonymous with CIF in the international cargo trade, its terms differ from the latter in a number of ways. Generally, the seller's risks are greater in a delivered transaction, since the buyer pays on the basis of landed quality/quantity. Risk and title are borne by the seller until such time as the oil passes from shipboard into the connecting flange of the buyer's shore installation. Also, the seller is responsible for clearance through customs and payment of all duties. Any in-transit contamination or loss of cargo is the liability of the seller. In delivered transactions the buyer pays only for the quantity of oil actually received in storage.

**Delivery.** The satisfaction of a futures contract position through the tendering and receipt of the actual commodity.

**Delivery month.** The month specified in a given futures contract for delivery of the actual spot or cash commodity.

**Delivery notice.** A notice presented through an exchange's clearinghouse by a clearing member advising of the intention to deliver the actual commodity in satisfaction of contract obligations.

**Delivery point.** Those locations designated by an exchange at which delivery may be made in fulfillment of contract terms.

**Delta.** The sensitivity of an option's value to a change in the price of the underlying futures contract, also referred to as an option's futures-equivalent position. Deltas are positive for bullish options positions, or calls, and negative for bearish options positions, or puts. Deltas of deep in-the-money options are approximately equal to one; deltas of at-the-money options are 0.5; and deltas of deep out-of-the-money options approach zero.

**Delta neutral spread.** A spread where the total delta position on the long side and the total delta position on the short side add up to approximately zero. Also known as neutral spread.

**Demurrage.** Compensation paid for detention of a ship during loading or unloading beyond the scheduled time of departure.

**Derivative.** Financial instrument derived from a cash market commodity, futures contract, or other financial instrument. Derivatives can be traded on regulated exchange markets or over-the-counter.

**Diesel fuel.** Distillate fuel oil used in compression-ignition engines.

**Differentials.** Price differences between classes, grades and locations of different stocks of the same commodity.

**Dirty cargo.** Those petroleum products which leave significant amounts of residue in tanks. Generally applied to crude oil and residual fuel.

**Discretionary account.** An arrangement by which the holder of an account gives written power of attorney to someone else, often a broker, to buy or sell without prior approval of the account holder.

**Distillate.** Liquid hydrocarbons usually water-white or pale straw color and of high API gravity recovered from wet gas by a separator that condenses the liquid out of the gas stream.

**Distillate fuel oil.** Products of refinery distillation sometimes referred to as middle distillates; *i.e.*, kerosene, diesel fuel, home heating oil.

**DOE.** Department of Energy. The federal government agency engaged in establishing policies and programs relating to national energy matters.

**Downstream.** An industry term referring to commercial petroleum operations beyond the crude production phase; refining, marketing.

**EFP.** Exchange of Futures for Physicals. A futures contract provision involving the delivery of physical product (which does not necessarily conform to contract specifications in all terms) to one market participant from another and a concomitant assumption of equal and opposite futures positions by the same participants to the physical transaction. An EFP occurs during the futures contract trading period.

**End-user.** The ultimate consumer of petroleum products; most commonly used in connection with large industrial or utility consumers.

**Escalation.** A clause, usually in long-term supply contracts, which provides for periodic price adjustment based on variations in any or all cost factors. "Escalating prices" are the opposite of "firm" prices, which are not subject to change over the life of a contract.

**European option.** An option that may be exercised only on its expiration date.

**Exercise.** The process of converting an options contract into a futures position.

**Exercise price.** The price at which the underlying futures contract will be bought or sold in the event an option is exercised. Also called the strike price.

**Expiration date.** The date and time after which trading in options terminates, and after which all contract rights or obligations become null and void.

**Extrinsic value.** The amount by which the premium exceeds its intrinsic value. Also known as time value.

**Feedstock.** The supply of crude oil, natural gas liquids, or natural gas to a refinery or petrochemical plant or the supply of some refined fraction of intermediate petrochemical to some other process.

**Fence.** A long (short) underlying position together with a long (short) out-of-the-money put and a short (long) out-of-the-money call. All options must expire at the same time.

**FIA.** Futures Industry Association.

**Fill.** The price at which an order is executed.

**First notice day.** The first day on which delivery notices may be delivered and authorized to an exchange.

**Floor broker.** An exchange member who executes orders for the accounts of others.

**Floor trader or local.** An exchange member who executes orders for his own account.

**FOB (free on board).** A transaction in which the seller provides product or crude oil at an agreed unit price, at a specified loading port within a specified period; it is the responsibility of the buyer to arrange for transportation and insurance and lift the material within the specified laytime.

**Force majeure.** A standard clause which indemnifies either or both parties to a transaction whenever events reasonably beyond the control of either or both parties occur to prevent fulfillment of the terms of the contract.

**Fractionation.** The process whereby saturated hydrocarbons from natural gas are separated into distinct parts or "fractions" such as propane, butane and ethane.

**Fundamental analysis.** The study of pertinent supply and demand factors which influence the specific price behavior of commodities.

**Fungible.** Interchangeable. Products which can be commingled for purposes of shipment or storage.

**Futures.** Standardized contract for the purchase or sale of a commodity, which is traded for future delivery under the provisions of exchange regulations.

**Gamma.** The sensitivity of an option's delta to changes in the price of the underlying futures contract.

**Gas oil.** European designation for No. 2 heating oil and diesel fuel.

**Gigajoule (GJ).** One billion joules, approximately equal to 948,211 British thermal units.

**Good till canceled.** An order to be held by a broker until it can be filled or until canceled.

**Heating oil.** Synonymous with No. 2 fuel oil, a distillate fuel oil for domestic heating use, or in moderate capacity commercial-industrial burners.

**Heavy crude.** Crude oil with a high specific gravity and a low API gravity due to the presence of a high proportion of heavy hydrocarbon fractions.

**Hedge ratio.** 1) Ratio of the value of futures contracts purchased or sold to the value of the cash commodity being hedged, a computation necessary to minimize basis risk. 2) The ratio, determined by an option's delta, of futures to options required to establish a riskless position. For example, if a $1/barrel change in the underlying crude oil futures price leads to a $0.25/barrel change in the option premium, the hedge ratio is 4 (four options contracts for each futures contract).

**Hedging.** The simultaneous initiation of equal and opposite positions in the cash and futures markets. Hedging is employed as a form of financial protection against adverse price movement in the cash market.

**Historical volatility.** The annualized standard deviation of % changes in futures prices over a specific period. It is an indication of past volatility in the marketplace.

**Horizontal spread.** Calendar or time spread.

**Implied volatility.** A measurement of the market's expected price range of the underlying commodity futures based on the market-traded option premiums.

**Independent.** Term generally applied to a nonintegrated oil company, usually active in only one or two sectors of the industry. An independent marketer buys product from major or independent refiners and resells it under its own brand name. There are also independents that are active either in refining or crude production exclusively and are not controlled by integrated oil companies.

**Independent power producer (IPP).** A non-utility power generating company that is not a qualified facility.

**Integration.** A term which describes the degree in and to which one given company participates in all phases of the petroleum industry.

**In-the-money.** An option that can be exercised and immediately closed out against the underlying market for a cash credit. The option is in-the-money if the underlying futures price is above a call option's strike price, or below a put option's strike price.

**Intrinsic value.** The amount by which an option is in-the-money. An option which is not in-the-money has no intrinsic value. For calls, intrinsic value equals the difference between the underlying futures price and the option's strike price. For puts, intrinsic value equals the option's strike price minus the underlying futures price. Intrinsic value is never less than zero.

**Inverted market.** A futures market in which nearby months are trading at a premium to distant months. See *Backwardation*.

**In-well transfer.** An inventory transfer of propane held in underground caverns or storage.

**Jet fuel.** Kerosene-type; quality kerosene product used primarily as fuel for commercial turbojet and turboprop aircraft engines.

**Jobber.** A middleman, buying from refiners/distributors and reselling to consumers/small distributors.

**Landed price.** The actual delivered cost of oil to a refiner, taking into account all costs from production or purchase to the refinery.

**Last notice day.** The final day on which notices of intent to deliver on futures contracts may be issued.

**Last trading day.** The final day on which futures contracts may be traded. Any contracts left open following this session must be settled by delivery.

**Lifting.** Refers to tankers and barges loading cargoes of oil or refined product at a terminal or transshipment point.

**Light crude.** Crude oil with a low specific gravity and high API gravity due to the presence of a high proportion of light hydrocarbon fractions.

**Light ends.** The more volatile products of petroleum refining; *e.g.*, butane, propane, gasoline.

**Limit.** The maximum amount a futures price may advance or decline in any one day's trading session.

**Limit order.** A contingent order for a futures trade specifying a certain maximum (or minimum) price, beyond which the order is not to be executed.

**Liquefied natural gas (LNG).** Natural gas which has been made liquid by reducing its temperature to minus 258° Fahrenheit at atmospheric pressure.

**Liquefied petroleum gas (LPG).** Propane, butane or propane–butane mixtures derived from crude oil refining or natural gas fractionation.

**Liquidation.** The closing out of long positions.

**Liquidity.** A futures market is said to be "liquid" when it has a high level of trading activity, allowing buying and selling of futures contracts with minimum price disturbance.

**Local.** See *Floor Trader*.

**Locked market.** A market where prices have reached their daily trading limit and trading may only be conducted at that price.

**Long.** The market position of a futures contract buyer whose purchase obligates him to accept delivery unless he liquidates his contract with an offsetting sale; also, the holder of a long position in the market.

**Long ton.** An avoirdupois weight measure equaling 2,240 pounds.

**Major.** A term broadly applied to those multinational oil companies which by virtue of size, age, and/or degree of integration are among the preeminent companies in the international petroleum industry.

**Margin.** Funds posted during the trading life of a futures contract to guarantee fulfillment of contract obligations.

**Margin call.** The demand for additional (variation) margin, the result of adverse price movement and consequent erosion of equity.

**Market order.** See *At the Market*.

**Maximum price fluctuation.** The limit, as set by the rules of a commodity exchange, of the fluctuation in the price of a futures contract during any one trading session.

**Mcf.** One thousand cubic feet.

**Metric ton.** A weight measure equal to 1,000 kilograms, 2,204.62 pounds, and 0.9842 long tons. For approximate conversion purposes, there are about 7.46 barrels of No. 2 distillate fuel in one metric ton; 8.51 barrels of gasoline and 6.7 barrels of residual fuel.

**Middle distillate.** Term applied to hydrocarbons in the so-called middle range of refinery distillation; *e.g.*, heating oil, diesel fuels, and kerosene.

**Minimum price fluctuation.** The minimum unit by which the price of a commodity can fluctuate per trade on a commodity exchange.

**MMBtu.** One million British thermal units; one decatherm. Approximately equal to 1,000 cubic feet of natural gas.

**Mogas.** Industry abbreviation for motor gasoline.

**Motor gasoline.** A complex mixture of relatively volatile hydrocarbons, with or without small quantities of additives, which have been blended to form a fuel suitable for use in spark-ignition engines.

**Motor oil.** Refined lubricating oil, usually containing additives, used as a lubricant in internal combustion engines.

**Naked.** A long or short market position taken without having an offsetting short or long position.

**Naphtha.** A volatile, colorless product of petroleum distillation. Used primarily as paint solvent, cleaning fluid, and blendstock in gasoline production to produce motor gasoline by blending with straight-run gasoline.

**Netback.** Commodity futures term referring to the difference between the cost of crude oil and the selling price of the resulting refined products (heating oil and gasoline).

**Net position.** A position not offset by a countervailing position; *i.e.*, the opposite of a spread.

**NFA.** National Futures Association.

**Normal market.** A market is deemed "normal" when carrying charges are reflected in higher prices for increasingly distant futures contract months.

**Octane number.** A measure of the resistance of a fuel to pre-ignition ("knock") when burned in an internal combustion engine.

**Offer.** A motion to sell at a specified price.

**Offset.** The elimination of a current long or short position by the opposite transaction; a sale offsets a long position; a purchase offsets a short position.

**Oil.** Crude petroleum and other hydrocarbons produced at the wellhead in liquid form.

**OPEC.** The acronym for the Organization of Petroleum Exporting Countries, oil-producing and exporting countries that have organized for the purpose of negotiating with oil companies on matters of oil production, prices, and future concession rights.

**Opening price.** The price for a given commodity generated by trading through open outcry at the opening of trading on a commodity exchange.

**Open interest.** See *Commitment*.

**Open order.** A resting order that is good until canceled.

**Out-of-the-money.** An option that has no intrinsic value. For calls, an option whose exercise price is above the market price of the underlying future. For puts, an option whose exercise price is below the futures price.

**Overbought.** A technical opinion that the market price has risen too steeply and too fast in relation to underlying fundamental factors.

**Oversold.** A technical opinion that the market price has declined too steeply and too fast in relation to underlying fundamental factors.

**Paper barrels.** A term used to denote trade in non-physical (futures, forward, swaps, etc.) oil markets which gives a buyer or seller the right to a certain quantity and quality of crude oil or refined products at a future date, but not any specific physical lot.

**Par or basis grade.** The grade or grades specified in a given futures contract for delivery. A contract may permit deviations from the par grade subject to appropriate premiums or discounts.

**Petrochemical.** An intermediate chemical derived from petroleum, hydrocarbon liquids, or natural gas, *e.g.*, ethylene, propylene, benzene, toluene, and xylene.

**Petroleum.** A generic name for hydrocarbons, including crude oil, natural gas liquids, natural gas, and their products.

**Pin risk.** The risk to a trader who has sold an option that, at expiration, has a strike price identical to, or pinned to, the underlying futures price. In this case, the trader will not know whether he will be required to assume his options obligations.

**Pipeline.** A pipe through which oil, its products, or gas is pumped between two points, either offshore or onshore.

**Point.** The smallest unit of measurement of a futures price.

**Position.** The nature of a person's open futures,

**Posted price.** The price an oil purchaser will pay for crude of a certain API gravity and from a particular field or area. Once literally posted in the field, the announced price is now published in area newspapers.

**Premium.** The price paid by the buyer of a commodity option to the seller of the option.

**Prompt barrel.** Product that will move within three to four days.

**Pump-over.** Intra-, or inter-, facility transfer.

**Put option.** An option which gives the buyer, or holder, the right, but not the obligation, to sell a futures contract at a specific price within a specific period of time in exchange for a one-time premium payment. It obligates the seller, or writer, of the option to buy the underlying futures contract at the designated price, should an option be exercised at that price.

**Rack loading.** Delivery by truck.

**Rack price.** Transport truck price charged by a supplier to customers that buy FOB terminal.

**Rally.** An advancing price movement following a decline.

**Refiner–marketer.** A marketer of gasoline and/or heating oil who operates his own refinery.

**Refinery.** A plant used to separate the various components present in crude oil and convert them into usable products or feedstock for other processes.

**Residual fuel oil.** Very heavy fuel oils produced from the residue from the fractional distillation process rather than from the distilled fractions.

**Resting order.** An order away from the market, waiting to be executed.

**Roll-over.** A special straddle trading procedure involving the shift of one month of a straddle into another futures month while holding the other contract month. The shift can take place in either the long or short straddle month.

**Round turn.** The execution for the same customer of a purchase and sale which offset each other.

**Settlement price.** The official closing price of the day for each futures contract, established by the exchange as a benchmark for settling margin accounts and determining invoice price for delivery on that day.

**Short.** The market position of a futures contract seller whose sale obligates him to deliver the commodity unless he liquidates his contract by an offsetting purchase; also, the holder of a short position in the market.

**Short the basis.** The purchase of futures as a hedge against a commitment to sell in the cash or spot markets.

**SIGMA.** Society of Independent Gasoline Marketers of America.

**Specifications.** Term referring to the properties of a given crude oil or petroleum product, which are "specified" since they often vary widely even within the same grade of product.

**Speculator.** An individual who trades rather than hedges in commodity futures with the objective of achieving profits through the successful anticipation of price movements.

**Spot.** Term which describes a one-time open market cash transaction, where a commodity is purchased "on the spot" at current market rates. Spot transactions are in contrast to a term sale, which specifies a steady supply of product over a period of time. Also, "spot month" refers to the nearest futures delivery month.

**Spread (options).** The purchase and sale of two options which vary in terms of type (call or put), strike prices, expiration dates, or both. May also refer to an options contract purchase (sale) and the simultaneous sale (purchase) of a futures contract for the same underlying commodity.

**Stop-loss.** A resting order designed to close out a losing position when the price reaches a level specified in the order. It becomes a market order when the "stop" price is reached.

**Straddle.** Also known as a spread, the purchase of one futures month against the sale of another futures month of the same commodity. A straddle trade is based on a price relationship between the two months and a belief that the "spread" or difference in price between the two contract months will change sufficiently to make the trade profitable.

**Straddle (options).** The purchase or sale of both a put and a call having the same strike price and expiration date. The buyer of a straddle benefits from increased volatility, and the seller benefits from decreased volatility.

**Straight-run.** Refers to a petroleum product produced by the primary distillation of crude oil.

**Strangle (options).** An options position consisting of the purchase or sale of put and call options having the same expiration but different strike prices.

**Strategic Petroleum Reserve (SPR).** Stocks (currently, only crude oil) maintained by the federal government for use during periods of major supply interruption.

**Strike price.** The price at which the underlying futures contract is bought or sold in the event an option is exercised. Also called an exercise price.

**Strip.** The simultaneous purchase (or sale) of futures positions in consecutive months.

**Synthetic futures.** A position created by combining call and put options.

**Swap.** A custom-tailored, individually negotiated transaction designed to manage financial risk, usually over a period of 1 to 12 years. Swaps can be conducted directly by two counter-parties, or through a third party such as a bank or brokerage house.

**Tariff.** A schedule of rates or charges permitted a common carrier or utility; pipeline tariffs are the charges made by common carrier pipelines for moving crude oil or products.

**Technical analysis.** An approach to forecasting commodity prices which examines patterns of price changes, rates of change, and changes in trading volume and open interest, without regard to underlying fundamental market conditions.

**Theoretical value.** An option's value generated by a mathematical model given certain prior assumptions about the term of the option, the characteristics of the underlying futures contract, and the prevailing interest rates.

**Therm.** 100,000 British thermal units.

**Theta.** The sensitivity of an option's value to a change in the amount of time to expiration.

**Tick.** The smallest monetary unit in which the movement of price of a given commodity may be expressed in futures trading. *See Point.*

**TLP.** Term-limit pricing. An agreement on price between a supplier and a wholesaler or jobber that runs for a specific length of time.

**Trend.** The general direction of price movement.

**Turnaround.** The planned, periodic inspection and overhaul of the units of a refinery or processing plant.

**Vega.** The sensitivity of an option's value to a change of volatility.

**Volatility.** The market's price range and movement within that range. The direction of the price movement, whether up or down, is not relevant.

**Wet barrel.** An actual barrel of product already physically in storage at the time of a given transaction; as opposed to a "paper barrel" which appears only as a credit in an accountant's ledger.

**Wire house.** A firm operating a private "wire" to its own branch offices or to other firms; a commission house.

**Writer.** The seller of an option. Also known as the grantor of an option.

# BIBLIOGRAPHY FOR GLOSSARY

Commodity Futures Trading Commission. *Glossary of Trading Terms*. Washington, D.C.: CFTC 105P (Rev. 4—86).

New York Mercantile Exchange. *Glossary of Terms*. New York, New York, 1996.

Quorum Books. *Trading Energy Futures: A Manual for Energy Professionals*. New York, New York, 1987.

# Index

# C

# D

# T